P · O · C ·

DINOSAURS

SAUROPELTA

IGUANODON

MEGALOSAURUS
TOOTH

P · O · C · K · E · T · S

DINOSAURS

Written by
NEIL CLARK
and WILLIAM LINDSAY

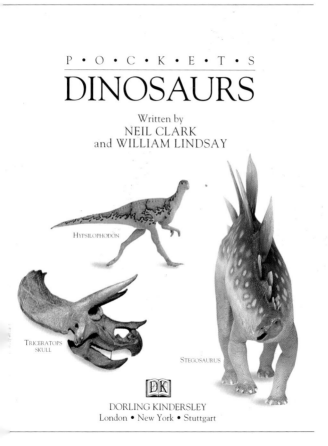

HYPSILOPHODON

TRICERATOPS
SKULL

STEGOSAURUS

DK

DORLING KINDERSLEY
London • New York • Stuttgart

A DORLING KINDERSLEY BOOK

Editor	Bernadette Crowley
Art editors	Ann Cannings
	Sheilagh Noble
Senior editor	Susan McKeever
Senior art editor	Helen Senior
Picture research	Caroline Brooke
Production	Louise Barratt

First published in Great Britain in 1995
by Dorling Kindersley Limited
9 Henrietta Street, Covent Garden, London WC2E 8PS

Visit us on the World Wide Web at http://www.dk.com

Reprinted 1996, 1997

A CIP catalogue record for this book is available from
the British Library

ISBN 0 7513 5177 6

Colour reproduction by Colourscan, Singapore
Printed and bound in Italy by L.E.G.O.

CONTENTS

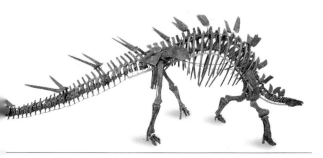

How to use this book

These pages show you how to use *Pockets: Dinosaurs*. The book is divided into several different parts: two on the main groups of dinosaurs, and one on non-dinosaur reptiles. There is also an introductory section at the front, and a reference section at the back. Each new section begins with a picture page, which sums up what it is about.

DINOSAUR GROUPS

The dinosaurs in the book are arranged into the two main groups of dinosaurs: saurischians and ornithischians. There is a separate section on non-dinosaur reptiles that swam in the sea and flew in the air at the same time.

CORNER CODING
Corners of dinosaur and reptile pages are colour coded with orange, blue, and green to remind you which group section you are in.

   SAURISCHIAN DINOSAURS

   ORNITHISCHIAN DINOSAURS

   REPTILES OF THE SEA AND AIR

HEADING
This describes the subject of the page. This page is about ceratopsian dinosaurs. If a subject continues over several pages, the same heading applies.

INTRODUCTION
This provides a clear, general overview of the subject, and gives key information that you need to know about it.

Corner coding

Heading

Introduction

ORNITHISCHIAN DINOSAURS

CERATOPSIANS
HORNS, BONY FRILLS, and a parrot-like beak were the trademarks of the ceratopsians. They were all quadrupedal herbivores, and many ceratopsians lived in great herds. Most ceratopsians can be divided into two groups. One group had short neck frills, the other had long neck frills. The ceratopsians were among the last dinosaurs to become extinct.

PSITTACOSAURUS
SKULL

*Psittacosaurus
may have moved
on all fours
when foraging*

Caption

PSITTACOSAURUS
This dinosaur was a 2-m (6½-ft.) long bipedal ancestor of the ceratopsians. It had a parrot-like beak and a very small neck frill, but lacked the horns of other ceratopsians.

Size indicator

CAPTIONS AND ANNOTATIONS
Each illustration has a caption. Annotations, in *italics*, point out features of an illustration.

8

These remind you which
section you are in. The
top of the left-hand page
gives the section name.
The right-hand page
gives the subject.
This page is in the
ornithischian section.

FACT BOXES
Many pages have fact
boxes. These contain
at-a-glance information
about the subject. This
fact box gives details
such as the size, key
features, and diet of
ceratopsians.

SIZE INDICATORS
These show the main
dinosaur/reptile on
the page next to an
adult human figure,
which represents 1.8 m
(6 ft).

*Fact
box*

*Running
head*

Annotation

LABELS
For extra clarity, some pictures
have labels. They may give
extra information, or identify a
picture when it is not obvious
from the text what it is.

REFERENCE SECTION
The reference section pages are yellow
and appear at the back of the book. On
these, you will find useful facts, figures,
and charts. These pages give dinosaur
records, such as the biggest and smallest,
and popular myths about dinosaurs.

INDEX
You will find an index at the back of this
Pocket Guide. This acts as a species and a
subject index. Every subject and type of
dinosaur covered in the book are listed
alphabetically.

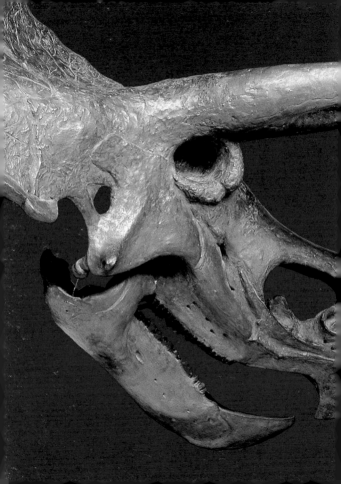

INTRODUCTION
TO DINOSAURS

WHAT ARE DINOSAURS?

ABOUT 225 MILLION YEARS AGO, a new group of reptiles appeared on Earth. Like all reptiles, they had waterproof, scaly skin and young that hatched from eggs. These were the dinosaurs. For the next 160 million years they ruled the Earth, before finally becoming extinct.

Powerful neck muscles were needed for ripping flesh from prey.

LAND LEGS
Dinosaurs were land animals – they could not swim or fly. All dinosaurs had four limbs, but many, such as this *Tyrannosaurus rex*, walked on only their two back legs, leaving the front legs free for other tasks.

Tyrannosaurus killed prey with its strong jaws and sharp teeth.

Clawed hands

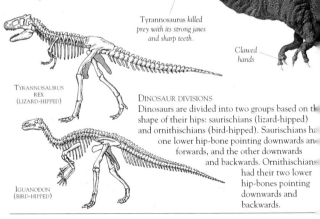

TYRANNOSAURUS
REX
(LIZARD-HIPPED)

IGUANODON
(BIRD-HIPPED)

DINOSAUR DIVISIONS
Dinosaurs are divided into two groups based on the shape of their hips: saurischians (lizard-hipped) and ornithischians (bird-hipped). Saurischians had one lower hip-bone pointing downwards and forwards, and the other downwards and backwards. Ornithischians had their two lower hip-bones pointing downwards and backwards.

Period	Millions of years ago	Examples of dinosaurs from each period	
CRETACEOUS	65-145		Triceratops
JURASSIC	145-208		Stegosaurus
TRIASSIC	208-245		Herrerasaurus

TIME LINES
Dinosaurs lived through
three periods in the Earth's
history – Triassic, Jurassic,
and Cretaceous. Different
species of dinosaur lived
and died throughout these
three periods.
Each species
may have
survived for only
2-3 million years.

*Waterproof
skin was covered
in scales*

*Muscular tail
balanced the front
of the body*

LIVING REPTILES
Modern reptiles, such as this iguana, have
many features in common with dinosaurs,
such as scaly skin and sharp claws.
But many scientists believe that
birds, rather than modern
reptiles, are the closest
living relatives of
the dinosaurs.

*Powerful
legs*

Types of dinosaur

Dinosaur designs were varied and
spectacular. A group of dinosaurs called
the sauropods were the largest land animals
that ever lived. The smallest dinosaurs were
chicken-sized. Large or small, all would
have been wary of hungry meat eaters. Some
dinosaurs had armoured skin for protection.
Others were fast runners
and could escape
predators by fleeing
to safer ground.

DINOSAUR TERROR
Tyrannosaurus rex and
other fierce meat
eaters had huge, sharp
teeth with which they
killed prey.

HERBIVORES
There were many more herbivores
(plant eaters) than carnivores
(meat eaters) in the dinosaur world.
A herbivore called *Stegosaurus* had
a sharp beak for cropping
leaves off plants.

ONE OF THE BIGGEST
Heavier than eight elephants and more than
24 m (80 ft) long, *Barosaurus*, a sauropod,
was one of the biggest dinosaurs.

*Barosaurus' tail
was about 13 m
(42 ft) long.*

Compsognathus
*reached just below
Barosaurus' ankle.*

Compsognathus *had long legs for running fast.*

See the size of Compsognathus compared to Barosaurus at the bottom of page 14.

Barosaurus' *extremely long neck was balanced by its very long tail.*

Rows of thick plates

ONE OF THE SMALLEST
Fully grown when only 1 m
(3 ft) long, *Compsognathus*,
a carnivore, was one
of the smallest
dinosaurs.

Sharp spines at the side

DINOSAUR FACTS

• There were about thirty times more herbivores than carnivores.

• The fastest dinosaurs were the theropods, which ran on two legs.

• Dinosaurs did not fly or live in the sea.

• The sauropods were the largest dinosaurs.

Thick legs

SPIKY PROTECTION
The plant-eating, slow-moving ankylosaurs had
armoured skin for protection from sharp-toothed
meat eaters. *Edmontonia* had bony plates and
spikes on its skin. It lived at the same time and in
the same places as *Tyrannosaurus rex*, so it needed
all the protection its armour could give.

More types of dinosaur

We will never know how many different
kinds of dinosaur existed over the 160
million years of their existence.
We do know that some
fossil remains belong not
to the dinosaurs but
to swimming and
flying relatives.

*Strong
plant-chewing
jaws*

*Arms
sometimes used
for walking*

*Iguanodon was
about 9 m
(29½ ft) long.*

*Iguanodon
travelled around
in herds.*

*Flexible
neck*

*Long
jaws*

VERY COMMON
Iguanodon was a common
dinosaur. In one
location, between
1878-81, coal miners in Belgium dug up
more than 39 *Iguanodon* skeletons

VERY RARE
Baryonyx is one of
the rarest dinosaurs
known. Only one
specimen of this
hook-clawed meat
eater has been found
so far

*A hooked
claw on
each hand*

*Baryonyx
walked on
two legs.*

*Baryonyx was
about 10 m
(33 ft) long.*

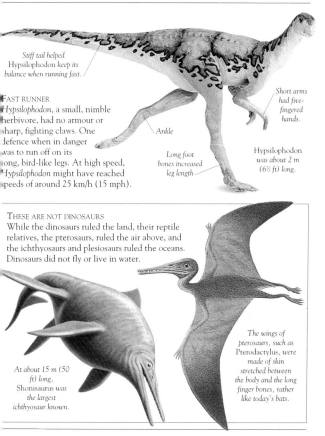

Stiff tail helped Hypsilophodon keep its balance when running fast.

FAST RUNNER
Hypsilophodon, a small, nimble herbivore, had no armour or sharp, fighting claws. One defence when in danger was to run off on its long, bird-like legs. At high speed, *Hypsilophodon* might have reached speeds of around 25 km/h (15 mph).

Short arms had five-fingered hands.

Ankle

Long foot bones increased leg length

Hypsilophodon was about 2 m (6½ ft) long.

THESE ARE NOT DINOSAURS
While the dinosaurs ruled the land, their reptile relatives, the pterosaurs, ruled the air above, and the ichthyosaurs and plesiosaurs ruled the oceans. Dinosaurs did not fly or live in water.

The wings of pterosaurs, such as Pterodactylus, were made of skin stretched between the body and the long finger bones, rather like today's bats.

At about 15 m (50 ft) long, Shonisaurus was the largest ichthyosaur known.

DISCOVERING DINOSAURS

SIR RICHARD OWEN
(1804-92)

EVERYTHING WE KNOW about dinosaurs is based on their fossilized remains. These are pieced together to make the skeletons we see in museums. Sir Richard Owen, the famous dinosaur expert, first named some reptile fossils as dinosaurs in 1841.

Fossils

Fossils are the remains of ancient living things buried and preserved in rocks. Most fossils were formed from tough body parts, such as the bones of animals or the woody parts of plants. Fossilization is a very slow process – it usually takes millions of years.

SAUROPOD
TOOTH

TOUGH TOOTH
Worn surfaces on fossilized teeth show how different dinosaurs ate in different ways.

SAUROPOD
EGGSHELL
FRAGMENT

FOSSIL EGGSHELL
Dinosaur eggshells, such as this fragment from a sauropod egg, were hard enough to be preserved as fossils.

FOSSILIZED
CONES

OLD CONES
These pine cones from the Cretaceous period were tough enough to fossilize.

IGUANODON
CALF BONE

FOSSIL BONES
Sometimes when bones fossilize, slow chemical processes capture every detail of their original inner structure and outer shape. Even when bones are cracked and crushed, it is possible to identify scars where muscles were attached.

STORY OF A DINOSAUR FOSSIL

1 The dinosaur *Struthiomimus* lies dead on a riverbank. For *Struthiomimus* to have a chance of fossilization, it must be buried quickly before it rots away.

2 Buried under many layers of sediment, over millions of years, the hard parts of *Struthiomimus* change to stony fossils.

3 Earth movements and erosion expose the skeleton at the surface. A scientist starts to chip away the surrounding rock.

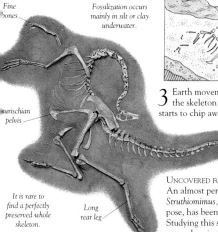

Fine bones

Fossilization occurs mainly in silt or clay underwater.

aurischian pelvis

It is rare to find a perfectly preserved whole skeleton.

Long rear leg

UNCOVERED FOSSIL
An almost perfect fossil of *Struthiomimus*, lying in its death pose, has been carefully uncovered. Studying this skeleton gives scientists more clues in the dinosaur puzzle.

Preparing dinosaurs

As scientists gain a better understanding of the way dinosaurs lived, museums try to arrange dinosaur skeletons in a variety of poses. Scientists at the American Museum of Natural History in New York built an exciting display. They showed a *Barosaurus* skeleton rearing up, defending its young against an attacking *Allosaurus*. As the fossil bones of *Barosaurus* were very fragile and too heavy to display in such a pose, a lightweight replica of the skeleton was made.

MAKING A MOULD
To make a mould of an original bone, liquid rubber is painted on to the surface of the bone and left to set. When the rubber has set, it is removed from the bone in sections. It is then supported by cotton gauze and surrounded with a plastic jacket.

POURING THE MOULD
The inside of the rubber moulds is painted with liquid plastic and strengthened by sheets of fibreglass. The mould sections are then joined together to recreate the bone's shape, and are filled with foam plastic.

Pouring the foam plastic into the bone cast

Filing away the rough edges of the joins

FINISHING TOUCHES
The joins in the cast bones are smoothed by filing. The plastic bones are then painted to match the colours of the original bone.

MOVING THE CAST

The skeleton is completed in sections before being mounted in its final position. As the casts are light-weight, it is quite easy to move the skeleton in large sections, such as the entire ribcage.

Several museum workers move Barosaurus' ribcage.

PLACING THE NECK

Barosaurus is mounted on a fibreglass replica of a natural landscape. The height of the *Barosaurus* skeleton rearing up is over 15 m (50 ft). The neck has to be lifted by a crane and placed carefully into its final position.

A guide rope steadies the neck as it is being raised.

The welded joints must be very strong to support the skeleton.

WELDING TOGETHER

A supporting steel frame runs through the skeleton sections. This frame was welded to join the sections together. The entire operation was carefully planned, since any mistake would have been very costly.

Dinosaurs on display

The most popular feature of many natural history collections is the dinosaurs. They are found in museums around the world. Scientists use these museums for storing fossils, and as laboratories for studying dinosaurs and other fossils.

STORING FOSSILS
The dinosaur fossils on display in museums are often just a fraction of the fossils the museum possesses. Sometimes thousands of fossils are housed in storerooms.

LIFE-SIZE SKELETON
Scientists and museum staff work together to construct a skeleton for display, such as this replica *Tyrannosaurus rex* skeleton. Full-size reconstructions of dinosaurs give us an impression of how they may have looked. This is particularly effective with awesome giants like *Tyrannosaurus*.

When running, Tyrannosaurus rex would have held its tail rigid for balance.

The back leg bones were thick to support Tyrannosaurus rex's enormous weight.

DINOSAUR DRAMAS
Many films and books portray dinosaurs and people as living at the same time, although dinosaurs became extinct over 64 million years before the first humans existed. Despite this inaccuracy, dinosaur films and stories make people more aware of these fascinating animals.

The large hips were the pivotal centre of the body.

Large chest cavity held the powerful heart and lungs

Leg bone is as tall as an adult human

PREPARING A SKELETON
Fossil dinosaur bones can be fragile and are often in pieces when first collected. Scientists use special tools to remove the rock surrounding a newly excavated fossil bone. This scientist is working on a *Triceratops* skull.

DINOSAUR WORLD

THE WORLD HAS NOT always looked the way it does today. Continents are constantly moving, and this very gradually changes the appearance of the Earth. The Triassic, Jurassic, and Cretaceous worlds all looked very different from one another. Mountains grew up; erosion wore land away, and plants and animals, including the dinosaurs, appeared and disappeared.

Changing Earth

The Earth's crust (outer layer) is made up of massive plates, which move on the semi-molten rock underneath. Over millions of years plate movement has caused continents to join together and separate to produce the distribution of land today.

Two plates colliding forms mountain ranges

The layer of semi-molten rock beneath the crust is called the mantle.

Molten mantle rock surfaces to form new crust.

MOVING PLATES
As the plates move, they either collide, which sometimes forms mountain ranges, or they move apart, forming new crust. When plates move apart, molten mantle rock rises between them, cools, and adds to the Earth's crust.

Edge of plate

The constant movement of the plates is called continental drift.

WORLD MAP OF PLATES

PLATE BOUNDERIES
There are nine main plates and several smaller ones. The plates are in constant motion, moving at a rate of only a few centimetres each year.

Land was joined together

Tethys Sea

TRIASSIC WORLD
In the Triassic period, when dinosaurs first appeared on Earth, all the land was joined together forming one gigantic continent. Scientists call this super-continent Pangaea.

Laurasia was made up of northern landmasses.

JURASSIC WORLD
In the Jurassic period, Pangaea gradually split into two continents. The continent in the north, made of large landmasses and smaller islands, is called Laurasia. The continent in the south is called Gondwanaland.

Gondwanaland

ometimes when two ates meet, one slides beneath the other.

This landmass became South America.

CRETACEOUS WORLD
Towards the end of the Cretaceous period, the continents broke up into smaller landmasses. Plates collided, forming the Rocky Mountains in North America and other mountain ranges.

Triassic world

The Triassic period was the beginning of the Mesozoic era, which lasted until the end of the Cretaceous period. The first dinosaurs appeared in the Triassic period. These dinosaurs were agile carnivores that evolved rapidly. Some became herbivores. Small mammals also appeared at this time, as did the flying reptiles, called pterosaurs.

ORNITHOSUCHUS

COELOPHYSIS

PLANT LIFE
The biggest trees were conifers. These formed huge forests, together with cycads and ferns. Squat cycads and ferns were ground plants fed on by smaller animals.

CYCAD

CROCODILES

PLATEOSAURUS

LIFE IN THE AIR

The pterosaurs were cousins of the dinosaurs, and were the only reptiles ever to fly. They flew above the conifer forests catching insects. They may also have skimmed the water of the rivers and seas for fish.

This pterosaur, Preondactylus, had a wingspan of about 1.5 m (5 ft).

MELANOROSAURUS

DICYNODONTS

PLATEOSAURUS

HERRERASAURUS

DINOSAUR LIFE

The number of herbivores, such as *Plateosaurus*, increased in the Triassic period. They were stalked by carnivorous dinosaurs, such as *Herrerasaurus*. Other reptiles lived alongside the dinosaurs, such as the pig-like dicynodonts.

Jurassic world

Early in the Jurassic period, the herbivorous dinosaurs were mainly prosauropods and small ornithopods. By the Late Jurassic, herds of giant sauropods roamed the land. These dinosaurs, as well as other reptiles and mammals, fed on the lush plant life. The first birds appeared, but the pterosaurs remained the rulers of the skies.

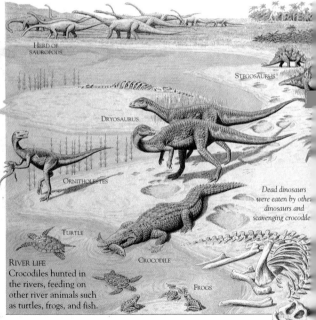

HERD OF SAUROPODS

STEGOSAURUS

DRYOSAURUS

ORNITHOLESTES

Dead dinosaurs were eaten by other dinosaurs and scavenging crocodile

TURTLE

CROCODILE

FROGS

RIVER LIFE
Crocodiles hunted in the rivers, feeding on other river animals such as turtles, frogs, and fish.

PLANT LIFE
Cycads, conifers, and ginkgoes
dominated the forests. Ferns and
horsetails provided a dense ground cover.

DINOSAUR LIFE
This was the age of the
giant dinosaurs. Herds of sauropods marched
across plains feeding from treetops. Fierce
carnosaurs, such as *Allosaurus*, preyed on herbivores
like *Stegosaurus*. Not all the dinosaurs were giants –
tiny *Compsognathus* also lived in this period.

Cretaceous world

In the Cretaceous period, North America, Europe, and
Asia were part of a much larger continent called Laurasia.
Carnivorous dinosaurs, which included the ceratopsians and
the hadrosaurids, browsed among marshy lowlands. The
giant sauropods became rare. In the Late Cretaceous
the terrifying tyrannosaurids appeared.
They were the top predators until
the extinction of the dinosaurs,
at the end of this period.

POLACANTHUS

CROCODILE

BARYONYX

CRICKET

BEETLE

DRAGONFLY

COCKROACH

DINOSAUR LIFE

Small herbivores were more common in
this period. Carnivores like *Baryonyx* m[?]
have lived on fish, while tyrannosaurids
probably fed on other dinosaurs.

PLANT LIFE

The Early Cretaceous landscape abounded in conifers
and ginkgoes, as in Jurassic times. Later in this period,
flowering plants and shrubs became common, as did
trees such as oaks, maples, and walnuts.

HERD OF
HYPSILOPHODON

IGUANODON

TURTLE

The herbivore
Iguanodon ate
leaves from conifers
and tall cycads.

Dinosaurs today

The remains of dinosaurs have been discovered on every continent, and new dinosaur fossils are constantly being discovered. They may be found by scientists on expeditions, by amateur fossil hunters, or by accident in places like building sites and underground mines. This map of the modern world shows the locations of the major dinosaur finds.

NORTH AMERICA
Expeditions are always being organized to search for dinosaurs in North America, since rocks from the dinosaur age are exposed over vast areas. The dinosaurs discovered here include:

- Allosaurus
- Triceratops
- Deinonychus
- Camarasaurus
- Parasaurolophus
- Corythosaurus
- Stegosaurus
- Apatosaurus
- Coelophysis

SOUTH AMERICA
Most South American dinosaurs have been found in Argentina and Brazil. Some of the earliest known dinosaurs have been found here. The South American dinosaurs include:

- Saltasaurus
- Herrerasaurus
- Patagosaurus
- Staurikosaurus
- Piatnitzkyosaurus

ANTARCTICA
The climate in Antarctica was much warmer in the dinosaur age than it is today. The bones of several small Cretaceous period dinosaurs have been found here, including a relative of the small ornithopod Hypsilophodon.

EUROPE
It was here in the 19th century that the first dinosaur fossils were collected and recorded, and where the name "dinosaur" was first used. Dinosaurs found in Europe include:

- Hypsilophodon
- Iguanodon
- Plateosaurus
- Baryonyx
- Compsognathus
- Eustreptospondylus

ASIA
Many exciting discoveries of dinosaurs have been made in the Gobi Desert. Scientists are still making new discoveries in China and India. Dinosaurs found in Asia include:

- Velociraptor
- Oviraptor
- Protoceratops
- Tuojiangosaurus
- Mamenchisaurus
- Gallimimus

AUSTRALIA AND NEW ZEALAND
There have been many fossil finds in Australia, and one in New Zealand. There are probably many sites rich in dinosaur fossils in these countries, but they have yet to be found. Dinosaurs found in these countries include:

- Muttaburrasaurus
- Leaellynosaura
- Austrosaurus
- Rhoetosaurus
- Minmi

AFRICA
Africa is a rich source of dinosaur fossils. A site in Tanzania has held some major discoveries. Dinosaurs found in Africa include:

- Spinosaurus
- Brachiosaurus
- Barosaurus
- Massospondylus

DINOSAUR ANATOMY

THE SIZE AND SHAPE of a dinosaur's head, body, and legs help us to tell one dinosaur from another, and also tell us how the body parts were used. From the skeleton inside to the scaly skin outside, each part of a dinosaur helps build a picture of these amazing animals.

Body power

The shoulder and pelvic muscles were crucial areas of power for light, fast runners as well as slow, heavy plodders. The largest dinosaurs were not always the mightiest. Some of the smallest dinosaurs were powerful runners.

Neck muscles

Pelvic muscles

Shoulder muscles

Rib-cage

Elbow joint

Thigh bone

PROTECTIVE CAGE
Like all dinosaurs, *Brachiosaurus* had a cage, formed from vertebrae, ribs, and sheets of muscle, to protect the vital internal organs.

Wrist joint

Shin bone

Toe bone

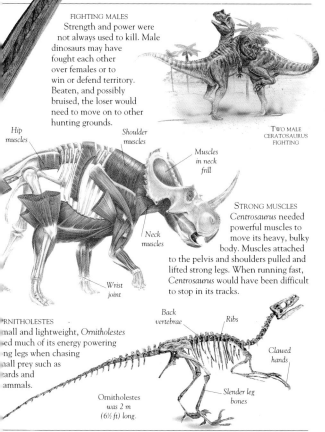

FIGHTING MALES
Strength and power were not always used to kill. Male dinosaurs may have fought each other over females or to win or defend territory. Beaten, and possibly bruised, the loser would need to move on to other hunting grounds.

TWO MALE CERATOSAURUS FIGHTING

Hip muscles

Shoulder muscles

Muscles in neck frill

Neck muscles

STRONG MUSCLES
Centrosaurus needed powerful muscles to move its heavy, bulky body. Muscles attached to the pelvis and shoulders pulled and lifted strong legs. When running fast, *Centrosaurus* would have been difficult to stop in its tracks.

Wrist joint

ORNITHOLESTES
Small and lightweight, *Ornitholestes* used much of its energy powering long legs when chasing small prey such as lizards and mammals.

Back vertebrae

Ribs

Clawed hands

Slender leg bones

Ornitholestes was 2 m (6½ ft) long.

Heads

Crests, frills, horns, and spikes adorned the heads of many dinosaurs. These decorations helped dinosaurs identify one another and were sometimes used for signalling. In a competition for territory, or control of a herd, the dinosaur with the most spectacular head might well have been the winner. Horned herbivores may have used their weapon for defence against hungry carnivores.

Large eye socket

Toothless jaws

BIRD BEAK
Gallimimus ate plants, insects, and lizards with its long, toothless beak. Its large-eyed skull looks very much like that of a big bird.

The size of the head crest may have been recognized as a sign of strength.

Strong jaws with beak

CENTROSAURUS HEAD

HEAD CREST
Oviraptors may have used their head crest to signal to one another. Although toothless, their beaked jaws may have been powerful enough to crush shellfish.

HORNS AND FRILLS
The Ceratopsian group of dinosaur had heads with a variety of frills and horns. These plant eaters probably used such decorations to frighten off attackers as well as to attract a mate.

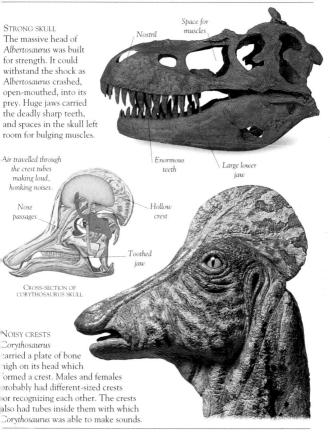

STRONG SKULL

The massive head of *Albertosaurus* was built for strength. It could withstand the shock as *Albertosaurus* crashed, open-mouthed, into its prey. Huge jaws carried the deadly sharp teeth, and spaces in the skull left room for bulging muscles.

Nostril

Space for muscles

Enormous teeth

Large lower jaw

Air travelled through the crest tubes making loud, honking noises.

Nose passages

Hollow crest

Toothed jaw

CROSS-SECTION OF
CORYTHOSAURUS SKULL

NOISY CRESTS

Corythosaurus carried a plate of bone high on its head which formed a crest. Males and females probably had different-sized crests for recognizing each other. The crests also had tubes inside them with which *Corythosaurus* was able to make sounds.

Necks

For dinosaurs, as with other animals, the neck was a vital channel between the head and body. Food passed from the mouth to the stomach through the neck; air was fed along the windpipe between the nostrils and lungs; nerves carried messages to and from the brain and body, and blood travelled through arteries and veins. All of these life-lines, as well as powerful muscles, were supported on the framework of neck vertebrae (neck bones).

BAROSAURUS
NECK VERTEBRA

LONG AND FLEXIBLE
Plant-eating, long-necked dinosaurs like *Barosaurus* probably used their flexible necks for cropping leaves from a large area of low-lying foliage while standing still. But if they needed to, they could have reached up to the leaves in tall trees.

Muscles were attached to spines on the vertebrae

STRONG AND LIGHT
The long neck of *Diplodocus* was made up of 15 vertebrae. These bones had deep hollows inside them to make them lightweight, although they remained very strong. A notch on top of the vertebrae carried a strong ligament which supported the neck in the way that wires support a suspension bridge.

Barosaurus' neck was 9 m (29½ ft) long.

SHORT AND STOUT

Allosaurus, a fierce and terrifying carnivore, had a short and stout neck. The neck bones were cupped tightly together to give a very mobile and curved neck. When *Allosaurus'* jaws bit into prey, powerful neck muscles pulled the massive head up and back, tearing chunks of flesh from the victim.

Curved neck

Powerful jaws with huge, sharp teeth

LIKE AN OSTRICH

Gallimimus held its head high above its shoulders, like an ostrich. In this position, *Gallimimus* could swivel its head on its long neck to give good vision in all directions.

The skull may have weighed as much as 51 kg (113 lb).

Very short neck

Long, flexible neck

HEAD SUPPORT

Triceratops had an extension at the back of its skull made of solid bone. This made the skull very heavy. A short and very strong neck was needed to support the huge weight.

Dinosaur limbs

Dinosaurs held their legs directly beneath the body, unlike other reptiles, which crawl with their legs held out from the sides of the body. Huge plant-eating dinosaurs, such as *Diplodocus*, walked on all fours with front and rear legs supporting bulky bodies. Most carnivores, such as *Albertosaurus*, walked on the two back legs, leaving the front limbs free for catching and holding prey.

IGUANODON FOOT BONE

Femur (thigh bone)

Knee

Muscle

Ankle

Metatarsals

Toe

MYSTERIOUS DINOSAUR
Almost all that is known of *Deinocheirus* is this huge pair of arms and hands. These forelimbs are 2.4 m (8 ft) long. It is thought that *Deinocheirus* belonged to a group of dinosaurs called ornithomimosaurs. The huge hands would have been used to catch and hold prey.

Long, slender arms

Fingers have 26-cm (8-in) claws

Three clawed fingers on each hand

FLESH AND BONE
The rear legs of *Albertosaurus* were powered by large muscles which pulled on the bones to make them move. The metatarsal foot bones worked as part of the leg, giving a longer stride.

Large claw
on first toe

Ankle
joint

Bird-like
toes

GOOD SUPPORT

Five widely spread toes on the rear
feet of *Diplodocus* helped support
the dinosaur's enormous weight.
The first three toes had claws. A
padded heel, like that of an
elephant, cushioned the
thundering footsteps.

Foot bone
extension

CHIOSAURUS

Elephants are
the biggest land
animals alive
today.

ELEPHANT

FLEET FOOT

Ornithomimus was one of the
speediest dinosaurs. Its three
foot bones were locked together,
making a long extension to the
leg. Running on the tips of its
toes, it could take long strides.
Ornithomimus may have reached top
speeds of 60 km/h (37 mph) – fast
enough to escape most predators.

LEGS LIKE PILLARS

The heaviest dinosaurs had pillar-
like legs, like those of elephants.
Brachiosaurus weighed about
50 tonnes (48 tons), so it
needed thick, strong legs
to support
its body.

More about limbs

The shape of a dinosaur's feet depended on whether it walked on two or four legs. Four-legged dinosaurs had similar front and rear feet, spreading their weight on hoof-like toes. Two-legged dinosaurs could use their front feet like hands, grasping at prey or holding plant food.

Long rear leg

Stout front leg

Hoof-shaped claw

Widely spaced toes

STOUT LIMBS
Widely spaced toes and thick, stout limb bones helped *Triceratops* spread the weight of its massive body. The shorter forelimbs carried the weight of *Triceratops'* huge head. Much of the body weight was supported by the long and powerful rear legs. Short and stubby toes on all four feet ended in hoof-shaped claws.

The claw was the first part of Baryonyx to be discovered, giving the dinosaur the nickname "Claws".

GIANT CLAW
The powerful carnivore *Baryonyx* had one of the largest dinosaur claws known. The curved talon, which was 31 cm (12 in) long, formed a huge weapon on *Baryonyx's* hand.

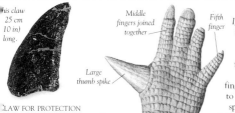

his claw
25 cm
(10 in)
long.

CLAW FOR PROTECTION
patosaurus, a giant sauropod
inosaur, had a pointed claw
n each front foot, which it
ay have used for defence.

Middle
fingers joined
together

Large
thumb spike

Fifth
finger

IGUANODON HAND
Iguanodon could use
its hands in several
ways. It could use
the hoofed middle
fingers for walking,
and the long fifth
fingers could hook on
to plants. The thumb
spikes were probably
defensive weapons used
for stabbing enemies.

PRESERVED
IGUANODON
FOOTPRINT

UANODON
OSSILIZED
OT BONES

The broad, three-toed
footprint matches the
fossilized foot bones.

NOSAUR PRINT
zanodon left many clues behind
en it became extinct. When it walked
damp sand or mud it left footprints,
ich dried and became preserved. The
otprints of an adult *Iguanodon* would have
en about 90 cm (35 in) long.

Tails

Dinosaur tails had many uses, and tail bones can tell us a lot about their owners. Flexible tails ending with long, thin bones were the trademark of the giant sauropod dinosaurs. Dinosaurs which ran on two legs had tail bones which locked stiffly together to help give balance. Tails ending in lumps and spikes were used as weapons against attacking enemies.

Deinonychus could run very fast when chasing prey.

Tail bones tightly locked together

BALANCING ACT

Scientists once believed that *Parasaurolophus* used its thick tail for swimming by sweeping it from side to side like a fish's tail. But they now think that the tail counterbalanced the front of the body.

TAIL WH

When defending itself, *Diplodocus* used its long tail like huge whip to swipe at its attacker. The tail had 73 bon joined together, and made a powerful weapon with i thin, whiplike endin

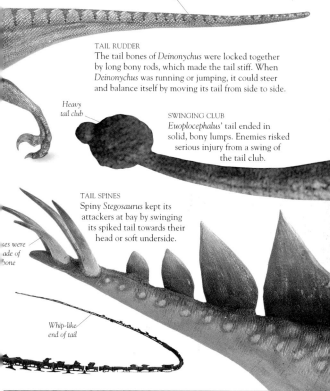

Tail held stiffly behind body

TAIL RUDDER
The tail bones of *Deinonychus* were locked together by long bony rods, which made the tail stiff. When *Deinonychus* was running or jumping, it could steer and balance itself by moving its tail from side to side.

Heavy tail club

SWINGING CLUB
Euoplocephalus' tail ended in solid, bony lumps. Enemies risked serious injury from a swing of the tail club.

TAIL SPINES
Spiny *Stegosaurus* kept its attackers at bay by swinging its spiked tail towards their head or soft underside.

...kes were ...ade of ...bone

Whip-like end of tail

Skin

Lizards and snakes, crocodiles and turtles – all have the tough scaly skin which is a trademark of reptiles. Dinosaurs were no exception. Their skin, preserved long enough in silt or clay to leave fossilized imprints, shows patterns of large and small lumps. Some dinosaurs, like the ankylosaurs, had spikes and plates of bone embedded in their thick skin – armour against attack from more dangerous dinosaurs.

SKIN SHAPE
Bony nodules, such as this one, were embedded in the skin of the armoured dinosaur *Polacanthus*.

WELL ARMOURED
Polacanthus had a protective coat of nodules and overlapping bony plates. Such tough armour would have deterred hungry enemies.

Bony nodule

CROCODILE SCALES
Crocodiles have a tough and leathery skin of lumpy scales. Just below the skin along the back, large bony plates, called scutes, add to the skin's toughness. The skin of crocodiles and other reptiles is also waterproof, keeping body moisture in but water out.

Crocodile skin in close-up

BONY PLATE
Ankylosaurs were among the most nobbly-skinned of the dinosaurs. Large bony plates, like this one, lay side by side forming a thick armour along the upper part of the body.

FOSSIL
ANKYLOSAUR
NODULE

Nodules were ridged in the middle.

NODULES AND SPIKES
Euoplocephalus had bony nodules set into its leathery skin. Pointed spikes across the shoulders gave added protection.

Shoulder spike

EUOPLOCEPHALUS

WRAPPED IN SKIN
In rare cases, a dinosaur's dead body dried and shrivelled instead of rotting away. This *Edmontosaurus* fossil has the skin impression preserved and wrapped around the skeleton.

Small bumps

SKIN PATTERN
Corythosaurus had no protective armour. Its skin, a mosaic of small bumpy scales, was wrinkled and folded around the moving parts of the body.

This fossil is 65 million years old.

DINOSAUR LIFESTYLES

ALTHOUGH DINOSAURS died out 65 million years ago, we know a lot about their lifestyles. Herbivores and carnivores lived in the world of dinosaurs. Some dinosaurs cared for their young. But whether they were warm- or cold-blooded has yet to be established.

Carnivores

Most carnivores had deadly sharp teeth and claws. Some hunted in packs; some hunted alone; while others may have scavenged on dead animals which were possibly killed by disease.

FAST FOOD
Dromaeosaurus had features common to many carnivores. It was fast, agile, and armed with sharp teeth and claws. *Dromaeosaurus* may have hunted in packs, chasing and bringing down much larger animals.

Clawed hands gripped prey

Long, slender legs

Slashing talon flicked forward

Sharp, serrated teeth lined the long jaws.

Lethal claw

CUTTING CLAW

Like *Dromaeosaurus*, *Deinonychus* had a lethal weapon – a 15-cm (6-in) long curved claw on each foot. When *Deinonychus* caught prey, it flicked the claw forwards to cut deep into its victim.

BARYONYX

From the side, *Baryonyx*'s skull appears crocodile shaped. *Baryonyx* may have used its long and narrow snout for catching fish.

TERRIBLE TEETH

The teeth of carnivorous dinosaurs were sharp with serrated (sawlike) edges for cutting through flesh and bones.

LOWER JAW OF
ALBERTOSAURUS

MEATY DIET

Tyrannosaurus rex was perhaps the fiercest carnivore. With its powerful body and massive head, it overwhelmed victims, delivering a fatal, biting blow with its deadly jaws.

Small hands could tear food apart

Herbivores

Plant-eating dinosaurs had to eat large
amounts of plants every day to fuel their
bodies. A herbivore's special diet needed
special ways of eating and digesting
food. Some herbivores' teeth were
shaped for chopping, raking, or
crushing. Other herbivores had
sharp beaks for snipping leaves
and twigs. Once swallowed,
these tough plants may have
taken days to digest.

GRINDING GUT
Barosaurus did
not chew its food –
it swallowed tough
leaves and twigs
whole. In a part of its
stomach, stones called
gastroliths ground the
food for digestion.

SMOOTH STONES
Gastroliths have been
found near the skeletons
of several dinosaurs.

HERBIVORE FACTS

• All ornithischian
dinosaurs were
herbivores.

• Some herbivores had
up to 960 teeth.

• There were no
flowers for dinosaurs
to eat until about 125
million years ago.

• Herds of herbivores
may have migrated
during dry seasons to
find fresh food supplies.

• Some of the plants
the dinosaurs ate, such
as pine trees, ferns, and
cycads, still grow today.

PLANT PULP
Edmontosaurus had hundreds of tough teeth packed together in its upper and lower jaws. The two sets of teeth worked together like a pair of coarse files, grinding leaves, fruits, and seeds.

Lever for muscle attachment

EDMONTOSAURUS LOWER JAW

Toothless front of jaw

Teeth packed together

Serrated cutting edge

PARASAUROLOPHUS

Parasaurolophus had hundreds of teeth for chewing tough ferns.

Root of tooth

LEAF CUTTERS
The teeth of sauropods such as *Rebbachisaurus* were designed for cutting rather than chewing.

TOUGH TO EAT
We can see which plants were available to dinosaurs by studying plant fossils. Herbivores such as *Parasaurolophus* had strong teeth for chewing tough plants such as ferns and conifers.

MAGNOLIA

GINKGO

MONKEY PUZZLE CONIFER

DINOSAUR MENU
Many of the plants the dinosaurs ate can be seen in gardens and parks today.

Senses

Well-developed sight, smell, and hearing were crucial to the dinosaurs' long-running success. Dinosaurs used these vital senses daily for survival in their hostile world. Dinosaurs that were active hunters tracked prey by following noises and scents. Many dinosaurs lived in groups and protected their young by listening and watching for predators.

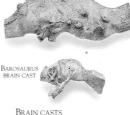

TYRANNOSAURUS REX BRAIN CAST

BAROSAURUS BRAIN CAST

BRAIN CASTS
Tyrannosaurus rex's brain was bigger than *Barosaurus*'. Brains are too soft to fossilize, but casts from the inside of dinosaur skull show us their shapes and sizes.

CROSS-SECTION OF SKULL OF PARASAUROLOPHUS

Long air passages

Teeth

Nasal opening where air enters

SKULL OF PARASAUROLOPHUS

Crest was 1 m (3 ft) long

MAKING NOISES
Parasaurolophus and other crested dinosaurs could produce noisy signals from their head crests, identifying themselves to each other or warning of danger. Tubular sound chambers ran from the nose of *Parasaurolophus* up into its crest. Air travelled through this prehistoric "trombone", where it vibrated as sound.

COLOUR

VIEW FROM LEFT

VIEW FROM RIGHT

BLACK AND WHITE

VIEW FROM LEFT

VIEW FROM RIGHT

DOUBLE VISION

We do not know if dinosaurs could see in colour, but eye position affected the kind of image seen. Eyes on the sides of the head, common in herbivores, sent two different pictures to the brain.

COLOUR

SINGLE VISION

Brain size is not always a sign of intelligence, but big-brained *Troodon* was probably one of the smartest dinosaurs. *Troodon* had large eyes and good vision. It benefitted from stereoscopic sight, which means it saw one image, the way that we do. Whether it could see in colour or black and white, *Troodon* could judge distance when chasing or catching its prey.

BLACK AND WHITE

Warm and cold blood

Reptiles are cold-blooded, which means that they depend on conditions outside their body, such as the Sun's heat, for temperature control. Warm-blooded animals, such as mammals, produce heat from food energy, have hair for warmth, and sweat to cool down. Although dinosaurs were reptiles, much of their behaviour, such as agile running, has more in common with mammals. Scientists are therefore puzzled over whether dinosaurs were warm- or cold-blooded.

Blood vessels

CROSS-SECTION OF
MAMMAL BONE

Blood vessels

CROSS-SECTION OF
REPTILE BONE

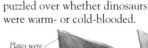

Plates were pointed at the top

BLOOD AND BONES
Dinosaurs had bones more like mammals than reptiles. Mammal bones contain far more blood vessels than reptile bones.

Cross-section: hole for blood vessel

Side view: blood vessels passed through holes in the bony plate

BACK PLATES
Stegosaurus used its back plates for warming up and cooling down. To warm up, *Stegosaurus* stood with its side to the Sun to heat the blood as it flowed through the plates. To cool down, it stood in the shade and lost heat through the plates.

COLD-BLOODED SUNBATHER

A typical cold-blooded creature, such as a lizard, spends hours sunbathing to raise the body's temperature to a level where it can work effectively. To avoid overheating, the lizard can cool off in the shade. When it is cold at night, or in the winter, reptiles are inactive.

Lizard sunbathing

High blood pressure was needed to reach a brain 15 m (50 ft) above the ground.

GOOD EXAMPLE

Dromaeosaurus is one of the best arguments for dinosaurs being warm-blooded animals. Fast-moving and agile, *Dromaeosaurus* had a lifestyle better suited to warm-blooded killers like wolves rather than reptiles like lizards.

BLOOD PRESSURE

Tall dinosaurs needed high blood pressure to pump blood to their brain. But down at the level of their lungs, such high pressure would be fatal. Warm-blooded animals have a twin pressure system. Perhaps dinosaurs had a similar system.

BRACHIOSAURUS

Eggs, nests, and young

Dinosaurs laid eggs, like most other reptiles as
well as birds. In recent years, scientists have
discovered dinosaur nesting sites which gave
them an insight into the early life of dinosaurs.
These sites showed that some young stayed in
their nests, cared for by adults, until they were
old enough to leave. They also showed that
dinosaurs, like many birds, used the same
nesting sites year after year.

EGG FIND
The discovery of
clutches of *Proto-
ceratops* eggs was the
first evidence that
dinosaurs had nests.
The shell of each egg
had tiny passages for air
to reach the young
dinosaur inside.

*Fossil egg with
broken eggshell
fragments*

*Young set
off in search
of food*

SMALL EGGS
These fossilized
sauropod eggs, which are
only 15 cm (6 in) in diameter, could have
produced young which grew to an adult length
of 12 m (39 ft). It probably took sauropods
several years to reach their adult size.

HOME LIFE

Female *Maiasaura* laid about 25 eggs in a nest which was dug in the ground and lined with leaves and twigs. Young *Maiasaura* were about 30 cm (12 in) long when they hatched. They were reared in the nest until they grew to about 1.5 m (5 ft), when they would be old enough to start fending for themselves.

FOSSILIZED MAIASAURA EGG AND SKELETON OF YOUNG

Maiasaura hatchlings were very weak.

EARLY START

Unlike the *Maiasaura* young who were looked after by their mother for several weeks, *Orodromeus* young left their nests as soon they hatched from their eggs. The young *Orodromeus* would have been preyed upon by carnivorous dinosaurs, such as sharp-sighted *Troodon*.

Newly hatched Orodromeus leaving nest

THE FIRST DINOSAURS

SEVERAL GROUPS of reptiles
existed before the dinosaurs
appeared. One group was the
thecodonts. These were the
ancestors of the dinosaurs, and
they probably also gave rise to the
pterosaurs and the crocodiles. Like
the first dinosaurs, thecodonts were
large carnivores which had
straighter legs than other reptiles.
The earliest known dinosaur,
Eoraptor, first appeared 228
million years ago.

A VERY EARLY DINOSAUR
Eoraptor may have been
the first dinosaur. It was
discovered in 1992 in
Argentina. *Eoraptor* had a
crocodile-like skull with
sharp, curved teeth.

*Jaws were
lined with sharp
teeth*

*Long, stiff
tail*

*Long tail acted as a
counterbalance to the
front of the body*

STAURIKOSAURUS

Staurikosaurus
was about 2 m
(6½ ft) long.

*Long, bird-
like back legs*

FAST HUNTER
Speedy *Staurikosaurus* was one of
the first carnivorous dinosaurs. It
had long, tooth-lined jaws for
catching its prey, which it chased
on its long and slender back legs.

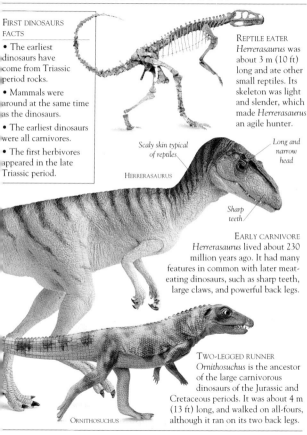

FIRST DINOSAURS
FACTS

• The earliest dinosaurs have come from Triassic period rocks.

• Mammals were around at the same time as the dinosaurs.

• The earliest dinosaurs were all carnivores.

• The first herbivores appeared in the late Triassic period.

REPTILE EATER
Herrerasaurus was about 3 m (10 ft) long and ate other small reptiles. Its skeleton was light and slender, which made *Herrerasaurus* an agile hunter.

Scaly skin typical of reptiles

HERRERASAURUS

Long and narrow head

Sharp teeth

EARLY CARNIVORE
Herrerasaurus lived about 230 million years ago. It had many features in common with later meat-eating dinosaurs, such as sharp teeth, large claws, and powerful back legs.

TWO-LEGGED RUNNER
Ornithosuchus is the ancestor of the large carnivorous dinosaurs of the Jurassic and Cretaceous periods. It was about 4 m (13 ft) long, and walked on all-fours, although it ran on its two back legs.

ORNITHOSUCHUS

DINOSAUR EXTINCTION

AROUND 65 MILLION years ago, the dinosaurs became extinct. At the same time, other creatures, such as the sea and air reptiles, also died out. There are many theories for this extinction. But, as with so many facts about dino-saurs, no-one really knows for sure what happened.

ASTEROID THEORY
At the end of the Cretaceous period a giant asteroid struck Earth. The impact resulted in a dust cloud which circled the globe, blocking out the sunlight and bringing cold, stormy weather.

Even the mighty Tyrannosaurus rex could not survive extinction.

SLOW DEAT[...]
The dinosaurs die[...] out graduall[...] perhaps over [...] period of sever[...] million year[...] *Tyrannosaur[...] rex* was or[...] of the la[...] dinosaurs [...] become extinc[...]

MAGNOLIA

FLOWERS

Flowering plants may have contributed to the extinction of the dinosaurs. Many of these plants would have been poisonous, and any herbivorous dinosaur that ate them may have died. Many carnivores, which fed on herbivores, would then have died because of lack of food.

VOLCANO THEORY

Many volcanoes were active during the Cretaceous period. There were vast lava flows in the area which is now India. This would have poured huge amounts of carbon dioxide into the air, causing overheating, acid rain, and the destruction of the protective ozone layer.

Crocodiles have not changed much in appearance over the years.

Megazostrodon was a mammal which lived in the Triassic period.

MAMMALS

Mammals appeared during the Triassic period, when they lived alongside the dinosaurs. They became the dominant land animals after the dinosaurs' extinction.

SURVIVING REPTILES

Crocodiles were around before the dinosaurs, and are still alive today. The reason these reptiles survived while the dinosaurs died out is a complete mystery.

SAURISCHIAN DINOSAURS

ABOUT SAURISCHIANS

THERE WERE two main
groups of saurischians –
the theropods and the
sauropodomorphs. The
largest dinosaurs, and
some of the smallest, were
saurischians. This group
differed from ornithischians
mainly because of the shape
of the hip-bones.

*Sharp-toothed
jaws typical of the
meat-eating
theropods*

SAUROPODOMORPHS
Members of the sauropodomorph
group were mainly herbivorous and
quadrupedal (walked on four legs)
The sauropodomorphs included
the largest of all dinosaurs,
Seismosaurus, which
was about 40 m
(130 ft) long.

TYRANNOSAURUS
REX

BAROSAURUS – A
SAUROPODOMORPH

COMPSOGNATHUS

THEROPODS
All theropods were carnivores, and were bipedal
(walked on two legs only). One of the smallest
dinosaurs, *Compsognathus*, and the largest ever
land-based carnivore, *Tyrannosaurus rex*,
belonged in the theropod group.

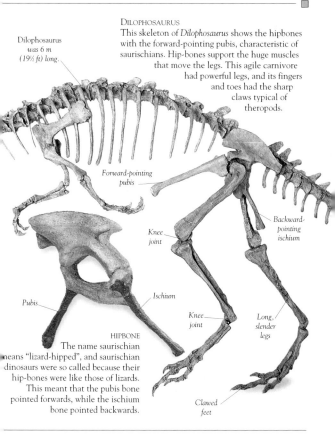

DILOPHOSAURUS

This skeleton of *Dilophosaurus* shows the hipbones with the forward-pointing pubis, characteristic of saurischians. Hip-bones support the huge muscles that move the legs. This agile carnivore had powerful legs, and its fingers and toes had the sharp claws typical of theropods.

Dilophosaurus was 6 m (19½ ft) long.

Forward-pointing pubis

Backward-pointing ischium

Knee joint

Pubis

Ischium

Knee joint

Long, slender legs

HIPBONE

The name saurischian means "lizard-hipped", and saurischian dinosaurs were so called because their hip-bones were like those of lizards. This meant that the pubis bone pointed forwards, while the ischium bone pointed backwards.

Clawed feet

THEROPODS

THE GROUP OF dinosaurs
called the theropods
were the killers of the dinosaur
world. Often large and ferocious,
these carnivores usually walked on
their clawed rear feet. Theropod means
"beast feet", but their feet were very bird-
like. Each foot had three toes for walking on,
with long foot bones that added to the length
of the legs. Sharp-clawed hands were often used for
attacking and catching hold of prey.

EARLY THEROPOD
Dilophosaurus lived during
the early part of the Jurassic
period. An agile predator
it was one of the first
large carnivorous
dinosaurs.

Tail

FOSSIL FIND
Coelophysis hunted lizards
and small dinosaurs. But
in this fossilized *Coelophysis* skeleton,
there are skeletons of young of the same
species among the ribs, indicating that
Coelophysis was
also a cannibal.

Coelophysis
*was 3 m
(10 ft) long.*

Bones of
*young in
ribcage*

THEROPOD FACTS

• All theropods were
carnivores.

• *Coelophysis* was
one of the first
theropods, living
about 220 million
years ago.

• *Tyrannosaurus rex*
was one of the last
theropods, living 65
million years ago.

• Many theropods
had no fourth or fifth
fingers.

• At least five
vertebrae supported
the pelvis of theropods

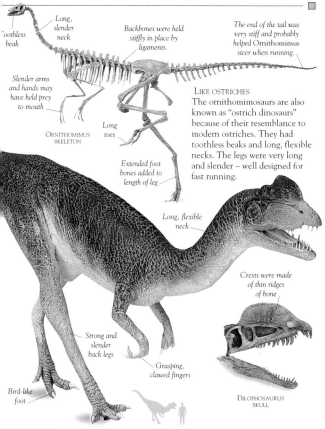

Toothless beak

Long, slender neck

Backbones were held stiffly in place by ligaments.

The end of the tail was very stiff and probably helped Ornithomimus steer when running.

Slender arms and hands may have held prey to mouth

ORNITHOMIMUS SKELETON

Long toes

Extended foot bones added to length of leg

LIKE OSTRICHES
The ornithomimosaurs are also known as "ostrich dinosaurs" because of their resemblance to modern ostriches. They had toothless beaks and long, flexible necks. The legs were very long and slender – well designed for fast running.

Long, flexible neck

Crests were made of thin ridges of bone

Strong and slender back legs

Grasping, clawed fingers

Bird-like foot

DILOPHOSAURUS SKULL

Carnosaurs

Of all the theropods, the ferocious carnosaurs are probably the most famous. Some carnosaurs could run as fast as 35 km/h (22 mph) on their large and powerful back legs. Massive heads carried a fearsome array of enormous serrated and curved teeth. *Tyrannosaurus rex* was the largest of the carnosaurs, and the most successful predator in the Cretaceous period. During the Jurassic period, *Allosaurus* was the top predator.

Small first toe

ALLOSAURUS FOOT
Like all other carnosaurs, *Allosaurus* walked on three large, clawed toes. The feet were strong as they had to bear the weight of the body. The first toe was small and faced backwards, off the ground.

Curved neck

Long, tooth-lined jaws could open wide to swallow lumps of meat.

Large, three-fingered hands had hooked claws

Front limbs were small and weak compared to the rest of the body

Ischium

Long foot bones increased leg length

SKELETON
Complete carnosaur skeletons are a rare find. There have been many finds of *Allosaurus* parts, including more than 60 skeletons in one quarry, so a complete picture of this powerful carnivore can be created.

ALLOSAURUS
About 145
million years ago,
Allosaurus was the
terror of sauropods,
ornithopods, and
stegosaurs. At about
11 m (36 ft) long, and
weighing as much as 2 tonnes (tons),
Allosaurus was one of the most common
dinosaurs during this time, and would
have been well supplied with prey.

Thick tail

Powerful legs for chasing prey

Tail was powerful and balanced front of body

Wider skull of Tyrannosaurus rex

Long and narrow skull of Allosaurus

SNOUT SIZES
Allosaurus had a
narrower snout
than *Tyrannosaurus
rex* and therefore
probably bit out
lumps of flesh
rather than making
bone-crushing
attacks on prey.

CARNOSAUR FACTS
• The oldest known
carnosaur is
Piatnitzkysaurus, from
the Jurassic period.

• Most carnosaur
species existed in the
last 10 million years of
the Cretaceous period.

• Carnosaur remains
have been found in
North and South
America, Asia, Africa,
Europe, and Australia.

• *Allosaurus* has been
known by more than
nine different names
since the first fossil
remains were found.

More carnosaurs

Fossilized remains of carnosaurs have been found worldwide. Many of the carnosaur skeletons that have been found are very incomplete. Consequently, they are difficult to study and understand, since pictures of whole dinosaurs have to be built up from small fragments of evidence. Scientists cannot even be sure that all of the dinosaurs they have grouped in the carnosaur family are, in fact, carnosaurs.

CARNOTAURUS
HEAD

Tail held out to counterbalance front of body

SPINOSAURUS
A large sail of skin supported on long vertical spines ran along the back of *Spinosaurus*. This sail is thought to have acted as a heat regulator, like the back plates of *Stegosaurus*. The sail may also have been used for recognition between rivals, or to attract a mate.

The spines were up to 1.8 m (6 ft) in length

Thick carnosaur tail

CARNOTAURUS

Found only in Argentina, *Carnotaurus* was about 12 m (40 ft) long. Its short, stubby head had the unusual feature of two pointed horns above the eyes. These horns may have been used as weapons when fighting rivals.

Rows of prominent, ball-like scales ran along the back and sides

Short, bony horns

Sharp, meat-eating teeth

FOSSIL TOOTH

This large carnosaur tooth belonged to *Megalosaurus* – the first dinosaur to be named in 1824. Many fossils have been wrongly identified as *Megalosaurus* remains, but very few real *Megalosaurus* fossils have been found.

The cracks occurred during fossilization.

Very short, weak arms cannot have been of much use

Powerful rear legs

ONE OF A KIND

The remains of only one *Eustreptospondylus* have ever been discovered. It is among many of the carnosaurs whose fossils were originally thought to belong to *Megalosaurus*. Like other carnosaurs, *Eustreptospondylus* would have walked on its three clawed toes.

Slender toes

Tyrannosaurids

Of all the carnosaurs, those in the tyrannosaurid family were the largest and probably the fiercest. The most famous member, *Tyrannosaurus rex*, was about 14 m (46 ft) long and 8 tonnes (tons) in weight. It is the largest land-based carnivore we know of. Tyrannosaurids not only caught and killed prey, they also scavenged dead creatures. They lived near the end of the Cretaceous period, and their remains have been found in North America and eastern Asia.

TYRANNOSAURUS REX TOOTH

Serrated edge

BIG TEETH
Tyrannosaurids had huge mouths, rimmed with huge, curved, serrated teeth. Some *Tyrannosaurus rex* teeth were 18 cm (7 in) long.

BIRD FOOT
The leg bones of *Tyrannosaurus rex* were thick and heavy to support its enormous weight. The metatarsal foot bones were locked into a single support, taking the weight above the three toes.

Knee

Tail raised for balance

Ankle

Metatarsals

Toe bones

Claws on end of toes

TYRANNOSAURUS REX
As the mightiest hunter, *Tyrannosaurus rex* would have had only another *Tyrannosaurus rex* to fear. But, like other animals, two *Tyrannosaurus rex* would have avoided confrontations, unless it was over females, territory, or food.

This hungry
Tyrannosaurus has
spotted another
Tyrannosaurus with
a meal.

ERRIBLE TEETH

Daspletosaurus had the massive jaw
ypical of the tyrannosaurids, capable
f delivering a deadly blow in one
ite. Flesh and bones were sliced
nd crushed by the
agger-edged jaw.

A loud roar
warns intruder
to stay away

A weaker
Tyrannosaurus
might retreat
rather than
risk injury.

A fight between two
Tyrannosaurus
would be a ferocious
and bloody battle.

Clawed feet
pin the food to
the ground.

7 3

Ornithomimosaurs

With their toothless beaks and slender feet, the ornithomimosaurs looked like giant, featherless birds. But their ostrich-like appearance also had the dinosaur features of clawed hands and a long tail. Ornithomimosaurs were long-necked and large – up to 5 m (16 ft) long. They were among the fastest dinosaurs, racing on slim and powerful rear legs. A wide mouth enabled them to swallow sizeable prey, such as small mammals, as well as insects and fruits.

ORNITHOMIMOSAUR FACTS

• The name ornithomimosaur means "bird-mimic reptile".

• Ornithomimosaurs may have run as fast as 70 km/h (43 mph).

• Predators: carnosaurs and dromaeosaurs

DROMICEIOMIMUS
This dinosaur had ten neck vertebrae which made a flexible stem for its large-eyed head. It used its slender arms and three-fingered hands for grasping or holding prey.

Knee joint

Ankle joint far up leg

Fingers were thin with long, sharp claws

Only the toes touched the ground

Long foot bones

Large eye sockets

LIKE AN OSTRICH
Struthiomimus had a similar running style to an ostrich. But unlike an ostrich, *Struthiomimus* had long, mobile arms which helped its clawed fingers grasp and hold prey. Its long tail was an important balancer at high speed.

Ostrich speed – up to 80 km/h (50 mph)

Struthiomimus speed – less than 50 km/h (30 mph)

Three locked foot bones

FOOT AND LEG
As in all other ornithomimosaurs, the feet and legs of *Dromiceiomimus* were built to give fast acceleration. Only the toes touched the ground – the foot bones were locked into a single, bird-like extension of the leg.

Sharp claws

Long, flexible neck

Mobile wrist

GALLIMIMUS
The largest ornithomimosaur was *Gallimimus*. It had a long and narrow, snouted head with large eyes for good sight. Its weak jaws were covered by a sharp, horny beak.

Oviraptosaurs

The first oviraptosaur to be discovered had a crushed skull and was lying on a nest of fossilized dinosaur eggs. The eggs belonged to a herbivore called *Protoceratops*. At the time of its death, the oviraptosaur was probably trying to steal the eggs to eat, and since its skull was crushed, it may have been caught and killed by an adult *Protoceratops*. Oviraptosaurs probably also ate berries and insects, as well as scavenging on the carcasses of dead animals.

FOSSILIZED NEST OF
PROTOCERATOPS EGGS

STEALING EGGS
Nests of *Protoceratops* eggs may have been a favourite hunting ground for hungry oviraptosaurs.

Head crest made of bone

Oviraptor philoceratops was about 2 (6½ ft) long

Ear

Bony prong

Tongue

OVIRAPTOR PHILOCERATOPS
This oviraptosaur had a short head with powerful, toothless jaws. Two bony prongs pointed down from the roof of the mouth. The prongs may have been used to crush eggs or the shells of freshwater molluscs.

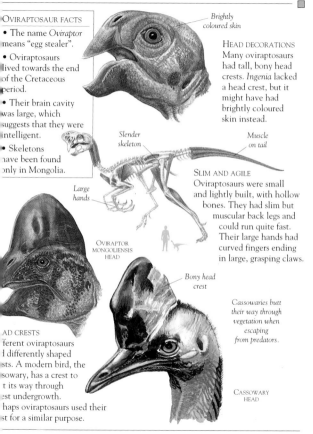

Brightly coloured skin

OVIRAPTOSAUR FACTS
• The name *Oviraptor* means "egg stealer".

• Oviraptosaurs lived towards the end of the Cretaceous period.

• Their brain cavity was large, which suggests that they were intelligent.

• Skeletons have been found only in Mongolia.

HEAD DECORATIONS
Many oviraptosaurs had tall, bony head crests. *Ingenia* lacked a head crest, but it might have had brightly coloured skin instead.

Slender skeleton

Muscle on tail

SLIM AND AGILE
Oviraptosaurs were small and lightly built, with hollow bones. They had slim but muscular back legs and could run quite fast. Their large hands had curved fingers ending in large, grasping claws.

Large hands

OVIRAPTOR MONGOLIENSIS HEAD

HEAD CRESTS
Different oviraptosaurs had differently shaped crests. A modern bird, the cassowary, has a crest to butt its way through forest undergrowth. Perhaps oviraptosaurs used their crest for a similar purpose.

Bony head crest

Cassowaries butt their way through vegetation when escaping from predators.

CASSOWARY HEAD

Troodontids

Near the end of the Cretaceous period, a very rare group of dinosaurs appeared. Scientists have called them troodontids. Although their body design was similar to the ornithomimosaurs, they were a distinct group of theropods. Troodontids had large brains for their body size. This, coupled with well developed senses, has given them the reputation as the most intelligent of the dinosaurs.

Slender head perched on long neck

Scaly skin

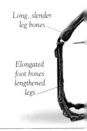

Serrated edge

TROODON
The best-known troodontid is *Troodon*. It had a light and delicate skeleton with slim rear limbs. Troodontid fossils are rare, partly because their thin bones were not easily preserved.

SHARP EDGE
Troodon had a long, narrow mouth lined with curved and serrated blade-like teeth.

Long, slender leg bones

FAST RUNNER
Troodon could run very fast on its long back legs. It probably chased small prey such as insects, small mammals, lizards, and baby dinosaurs.

Elongated foot bones lengthened legs

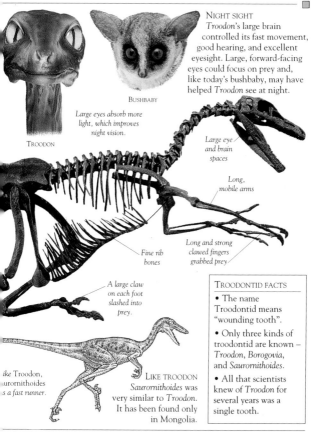

NIGHT SIGHT

Troodon's large brain controlled its fast movement, good hearing, and excellent eyesight. Large, forward-facing eyes could focus on prey and, like today's bushbaby, may have helped *Troodon* see at night.

BUSHBABY

Large eyes absorb more light, which improves night vision.

TROODON

Large eye and brain spaces

Long, mobile arms

Long and strong clawed fingers grabbed prey

Fine rib bones

A large claw on each foot slashed into prey.

ike Troodon, auromithoides s a fast runner.

LIKE TROODON *Sauromithoides* was very similar to *Troodon*. It has been found only in Mongolia.

TROODONTID FACTS

• The name Troodontid means "wounding tooth".

• Only three kinds of troodontid are known – *Troodon*, *Borogovia*, and *Sauromithoides*.

• All that scientists knew of *Troodon* for several years was a single tooth.

Dromaeosaurids

These razor-toothed carnivores were very agile, had large brains, and huge eyes with stereoscopic vision. They were among the most terrifying of all dinosaurs. A large sickle-shaped talon on their inner toes could rotate through 180°, slicing into their prey's tough hide.

Sharp teeth

Eye socket

Rigid tail

Some of the Deinonychus pack might die during an attack

DROMAEOSAURUS SKULL
The skull of *Dromaeosaurus* shows that it had sharp teeth, large, forward-pointing eyes for judging distance, and a large brain which suggests that it was intelligent.

DROMAEOSAURID FACTS

• The name dromaeosaurid means "swift reptile".

• They are thought to be among the most intelligent and agile of the dinosaurs.

• The largest were up to 2 m (6½ ft) tall.

• They lived in the Cretaceous period.

PACK HUNTING
Deinonychus hunted in packs, bringing down their prey with their sharp-clawed hands and slashing talons. A combined attack meant that they could kill prey much larger than themselves, such as the herbivore *Tenontosaurus*.

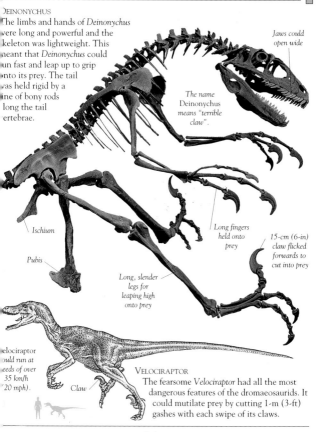

DEINONYCHUS
The limbs and hands of *Deinonychus* were long and powerful and the skeleton was lightweight. This meant that *Deinonychus* could run fast and leap up to grip onto its prey. The tail was held rigid by a line of bony rods along the tail vertebrae.

Jaws could open wide

The name Deinonychus means "terrible claw".

Long fingers held onto prey

15-cm (6-in) claw flicked forwards to cut into prey

Ischium

Pubis

Long, slender legs for leaping high onto prey

Velociraptor could run at speeds of over 35 km/h (20 mph).

Claw

VELOCIRAPTOR
The fearsome *Velociraptor* had all the most dangerous features of the dromaeosaurids. It could mutilate prey by cutting 1-m (3-ft) gashes with each swipe of its claws.

Other theropods

COMPSOGNATHUS
SKULL

There was a huge variety of theropods. Most have been put into groups, like the carnosaurs, but some theropods, such as *Baryonyx*, *Ornitholestes*, and *Compsognathus*, do not fit into any of the established groups. *Baryonyx* had an unusual, crocodile-like jaw, and a savage claw on each hand. *Compsognathus* and *Ornitholestes* were two of the smallest dinosaurs.

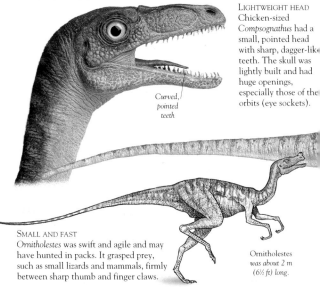

LIGHTWEIGHT HEAD
Chicken-sized *Compsognathus* had a small, pointed head with sharp, dagger-like teeth. The skull was lightly built and had huge openings, especially those of the orbits (eye sockets).

Curved, pointed teeth

SMALL AND FAST
Ornitholestes was swift and agile and may have hunted in packs. It grasped prey, such as small lizards and mammals, firmly between sharp thumb and finger claws.

Ornitholestes was about 2 m (6½ ft) long.

UNIQUE SKELETON
We know about *Baryonyx* from a single
skeleton, which includes a 30-cm- (6-in-)
long thumb claw. Its crocodile-like snout,
which had a crest on top, had 128
finely serrated teeth. The main
diet of *Baryonyx* may have been
fish, which it could snatch
from the river using its
long claws.

*Lower
jaw*

The Baryonyx
skeleton that was
found was only 70 per
cent complete.

*Clawed
foot*

BARYONYX
Baryonyx would have been about 10.5 m
(34 ft) long and nearly 3 m (10 ft) tall. It
held its head low, and its neck was straight,
not curved like many other theropods.

*Crocodile-like
snout*

*Neck held
straight*

DEATH POSE
This reconstruction
of *Baryonyx* shows
how it must have
looked shortly
after dying.

*Powerful
legs*

DINOSAURS AND BIRDS

SURPRISING THOUGH IT might
seem, scientists now recognize
birds as the closest living relatives
of dinosaurs. The most primitive
bird is *Archaeopteryx*. In 1861, an
Archaeopteryx skeleton together
with fossil impressions of its
feathers was found in a quarry in
Germany. *Archaeopteryx* lived
about 140 million years ago,
alongside the
dinosaurs which
it resembled in
many ways.

COMPSOGNATHUS FOSSIL
The fossil skeletons of
Compsognathus (above) a
Archaeopteryx look very
similar. Scientists found
Archaeopteryx skeleton in
1951, but for 22 years the
mistakenly thought it wa
Compsognathus skeleton.

Lightweight
skull

Short
body

Long
tail

Long,
slender
leg bone

Long
fingers

Elongated
foot
bone

COMPSOGNATHUS
SKELETON

Short
body

Lor
tai

SIMILARITIES
Small theropod
dinosaurs, such as
Compsognathus,
had many features
in common with
Archaeopteryx.
These included
a lightweight
skull, a short body, long, thin
limbs, and in some theropods, a
wishbone. This helps confirm
their close relationship.

ARCHAEOPTERYX
SKELETON

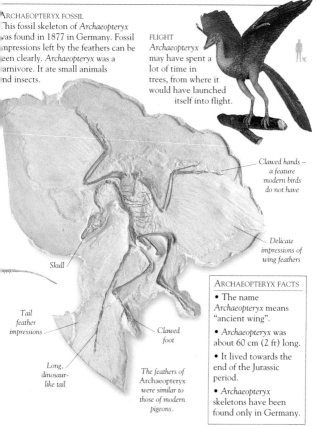

ARCHAEOPTERYX FOSSIL

This fossil skeleton of *Archaeopteryx* was found in 1877 in Germany. Fossil impressions left by the feathers can be seen clearly. *Archaeopteryx* was a carnivore. It ate small animals and insects.

FLIGHT
Archaeopteryx may have spent a lot of time in trees, from where it would have launched itself into flight.

Clawed hands – a feature modern birds do not have

Delicate impressions of wing feathers

Skull

Tail feather impressions

Clawed foot

Long, dinosaur-like tail

The feathers of Archaeopteryx were similar to those of modern pigeons.

ARCHAEOPTERYX FACTS

• The name *Archaeopteryx* means "ancient wing".

• *Archaeopteryx* was about 60 cm (2 ft) long.

• It lived towards the end of the Jurassic period.

• *Archaeopteryx* skeletons have been found only in Germany.

SAUROPODOMORPHS

TWO GROUPS, the prosauropods and the sauropods, are included in the sauropodomorphs. Unlike the theropods, most sauropodomorphs were quadrupedal (walked on four legs) and were plant eaters. They had long necks and tails, and ranged in length from 2 m (6½ ft) to 40 m (130 ft).

APATOSAURUS
THUMB CLAW

THUMB CLAW
Many sauropodomorphs had big, curved thumb claws. They probably used these dangerous weapons for defence.

Long, flexible neck

Large front feet could hold plants when feeding

Plateosaurus may have often walked on only two legs.

Prosauropods such as Plateosaurus were the first large land animals.

Small skull

PLATEOSAURUS
Several complete skeletons of the prosauropod *Plateosaurus* have been found. It is one of the earliest and largest saurischian dinosaurs of the Triassic period. Although quadrupedal, it could probably stand on its hind legs to reach up to feed on the higher branches.

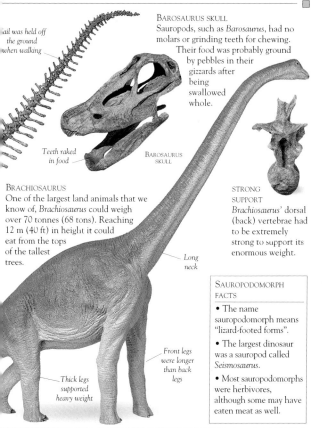

*ail was held off
the ground
when walking*

BAROSAURUS SKULL
Sauropods, such as *Barosaurus*, had no
molars or grinding teeth for chewing.
Their food was probably ground
by pebbles in their
gizzards after
being
swallowed
whole.

*Teeth raked
in food*

BAROSAURUS
SKULL

BRACHIOSAURUS
One of the largest land animals that we
know of, *Brachiosaurus* could weigh
over 70 tonnes (68 tons). Reaching
12 m (40 ft) in height it could
eat from the tops
of the tallest
trees.

*Long
neck*

STRONG
SUPPORT
Brachiosaurus' dorsal
(back) vertebrae had
to be extremely
strong to support its
enormous weight.

*Front legs
were longer
than back
legs*

*Thick legs
supported
heavy weight*

SAUROPODOMORPH
FACTS

• The name
sauropodomorph means
"lizard-footed forms".

• The largest dinosaur
was a sauropod called
Seismosaurus.

• Most sauropodomorphs
were herbivores,
although some may have
eaten meat as well.

Prosauropods

The prosauropods are thought to be the ancestors of the sauropods. Both groups have long necks and small heads, but the prosauropods were generally smaller in size. Most prosauropods were herbivores, although some may have been omnivores (eating both meat and plants).

MASSOSPONDYLUS
THUMB CLAW

THUMB CLAW
Massospondylus may have been an omnivore as it had large, serrated front teeth. It also had sharp thumb claws, which it may have used to attack prey, as well as for defence.

Teeth

Eye socket

SMALL SKULL
Riojasaurus, at 10 m (33 ft) in length, was the largest prosauropod. As with other prosauropods, its skull was tiny compared to its massive body, and its jaws were lined with leaf-shaped teeth for shredding plant food.

ANCHISAURUS
This prosauropod was designed to walk on all fours, but it may have occasionally run on two feet. *Anchisaurus* had large, sickle-shaped thumb claws which would have been dangerous weapons against attackers.

Slender back leg

VIEW FROM ABOVE
This view from above of *Anchisaurus* shows that its body was long and slender. It would have held its tail off the ground when walking.

Slim and flexible neck

REACHING HIGH
Plateosaurus was one of the earliest and largest saurischian dinosaurs. It grew to about 8 m (26 ft) in length, and could stand on its hind legs to reach tall trees when feeding.

Lower arm

Large thumb claw

Thumb claw

PULLING CLAW
The toes on the hands of *Plateosaurus* varied greatly in length. The thumb, the largest, ended with a huge, sharp claw.

Sauropods

The largest ever land animals were included in the sauropod group. Sauropods were quadrupedal, plant-eating saurischian dinosaurs. They all had huge bodies with long necks and elephant-like legs. They also had long tails which they used as whip-like weapons against enemies.

TAIL REINFORCEMENT
Tail bones like the one above were on the underside of *Diplodocus*' tail. They reinforced and protected the tail when it was pressed against the ground.

Peg-like teeth

Back of jaws was toothless

FRONT TEETH
Diplodocus had a long skull with peg-like teeth at the front of the jaws. The teeth would have raked in plants such as cycads, ginkgoes, and conifers. *Diplodocus* had no back teeth for chewing, so the food was probably ground in the stomach by gastroliths (stomach stones).

APATOSAURUS
This sauropod was once known as Brontosaurus. At 23 m (73 ft) long and weighing 27 tonnes (26½ tons), it was one of the largest sauropods. It had a long, horse-like head with a fist-sized brain, and powerful legs with padded feet.

Tail contained 82 bones

TAIL WEAPON
Barosaurus resembled *Diplodocus*, but had a slightly longer neck and a shorter tail. The narrow tail may have been a defence weapon.

Tail may have been used like a whip against enemies

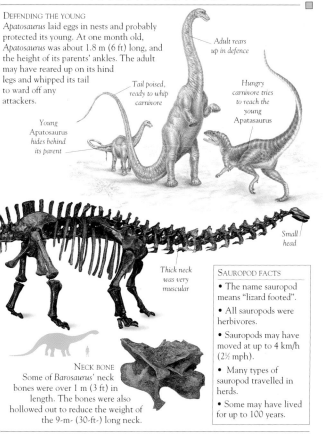

DEFENDING THE YOUNG
Apatosaurus laid eggs in nests and probably
protected its young. At one month old,
Apatosaurus was about 1.8 m (6 ft) long, and
the height of its parents' ankles. The adult
may have reared up on its hind
legs and whipped its tail
to ward off any
attackers.

*Adult rears
up in defence*

*Hungry
carnivore tries
to reach the
young
Apatasaurus*

*Tail poised,
ready to whip
carnivore*

*Young
Apatosaurus
hides behind
its parent*

*Thick neck
was very
muscular*

*Small
head*

NECK BONE
Some of *Barosaurus*' neck
bones were over 1 m (3 ft) in
length. The bones were also
hollowed out to reduce the weight of
the 9-m- (30-ft-) long neck.

SAUROPOD FACTS

- The name sauropod
means "lizard footed".

- All sauropods were
herbivores.

- Sauropods may have
moved at up to 4 km/h
(2½ mph).

- Many types of
sauropod travelled in
herds.

- Some may have lived
for up to 100 years.

More sauropods

Scientists used to think that the ankylosaurs were the only armoured dinosaurs. But the discovery of *Saltasaurus* proved that some sauropods had armour, too. It was also thought that sauropods may have lived in water, but we now know that the high water pressure at depth would not have allowed them to breathe.

SHORT SKULL
The short and high skull of *Camarasaurus* has a very large orbit (eye socket) and naris (nostril socket). There are approximately 48 spoon-like teeth.

Toothless snout tugged leaves from trees

SALTASAURUS
At 12 m (39 ft) long, *Saltasaurus* was quite small for a sauropod. Its armour consisted of large bony plates surrounded by smaller bony nodules. The armour possibly covered *Saltasaurus'* back and sides. The group of armoured sauropods is called the titanosaurids.

SEGNOSAURUS
This sauropod was an unusual dinosaur. It does not look like a sauropodomorph, and some scientists place it in a group by itself. Although *Segnosaurus* ate plants, it may also have eaten meat. Its hands had long, curved claws which it may have used to scratch at termite mounds.

Segnosaurus at termite mound

CETIOSAURUS
An early sauropod, *Cetiosaurus* had massive, heavy, and solid bones. Later sauropods had bones that were light and hollow.

Cetiosaurus was the first sauropod to be discovered.

Thick legs to support enormous weight

Cetiosaurus may have weighed as much as five elephants.

Bony nodules

NODULES
Only randomly scattered nodules of *Saltasaurus* have been found, so we can only guess at their position on its body.

Bony lumps

SKIN IMPRESSION
Parts of the body of *Saltasaurus* were protected by a covering of tightly packed, pea-sized, bony lumps.

ORNITHISCHIAN DINOSAURS

ABOUT ORNITHISCHIANS

THERE WERE FIVE main groups of ornithischian. They were all herbivores with hoofed feet and hip-bones arranged like modern birds. They also had beaked mouths, apart from those in the pachycephalosaur group. Ornithischians were either bipedal or quadrupedal. Bipedal ornithischians had stiffened tails to counterbalance their bodies while feeding or running.

CERATOPSIANS

ANKYLOSAURS

PACHYCEPHALOSAURS

ORNITHOPODS

FIVE GROUPS
The five groups of ornithischians were: ceratopsians, with their neck frills; ankylosaurs, with their body armour; pachycephalosaurs, with their domed heads; stegosaurs, with their back plates; and the bird-like ornithopods.

STEGOSAURS

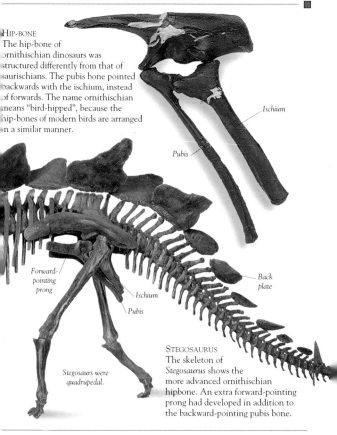

HIP-BONE

The hip-bone of ornithischian dinosaurs was structured differently from that of saurischians. The pubis bone pointed backwards with the ischium, instead of forwards. The name ornithischian means "bird-hipped", because the hip-bones of modern birds are arranged in a similar manner.

Ischium

Pubis

Forward-pointing prong

Ischium

Pubis

Stegosaurs were quadrupedal.

Back plate

STEGOSAURUS

The skeleton of *Stegosaurus* shows the more advanced ornithischian hipbone. An extra forward-pointing prong had developed in addition to the backward-pointing pubis bone.

STEGOSAURS

THE MOST NOTICEABLE features of the stegosaurs were the large plates, or spines, along an arched back. These plates may have regulated body temperature, and they may have also given protection, or even attracted a mate. Stegosaurs had small heads, and tiny brains no larger than a golf ball. The head was carried close to the ground for eating short, leafy plants and fruits.

Eye socket

STEGOSAURUS SKULL
The skull of *Stegosaurus* was long and narrow. It had a toothless beak and small cheek teeth for chewing vegetation.

TAIL END
Stegosaurus is the most commonly known of all stegosaurs. It had long, horny spines on the end of its tail. With a quick swing of the tail, these spines could inflict a crippling stab to a predator, such as *Allosaurus*.

Spines had a sharp end

PLATES AND SPINES
From above you can see the staggered plates along the top of *Stegosaurus'* body. This view also shows the tail spines pointing backwards and outwards – protection against attack from behind for when *Stegosaurus* was escaping.

Backward-pointing spines

Staggered plates

• The name stegosaur means "plated reptile".

• Stegosaurs ranged in size from 4.5 m (15 ft) to 9 m (29½ ft).

• The stegosaur group survived for over 50 million years.

• They ate only certain plants, probably seed ferns and cycads.

• All stegosaurs had tail spines for defence.

STEGOSAURUS
The plates on *Stegosaurus*' back would have been useful for display, for soaking in heat from the Sun, or when cooling off. The size of the plates varied greatly. They were tallest in the region of the hips, reaching about 75 cm (2½ ft) in height.

Plates were tallest above hips

FOSSIL PLATE
This fossil plate was one of the small plates at the front of *Stegosaurus*. The plates were thin and made of bone, and contained a network of blood vessels.

Small head

More stegosaurs

The front legs of stegosaurs were shorter than the back legs. It has been suggested that stegosaurs could have reared up on their hind legs, balancing with their tail. The supple tail and powerful rear legs could have formed a tripod allowing them to reach higher vegetation. The plates and spines may have been used for different purposes in different stegosaurs.

Cast of "second brain"

TUOJIANGOSAURUS
Some scientists believe this reconstructed skeleton of *Tuojiangosaurus* to be wrong. They think the front limbs should be straighter, and not bent like a lizard's.

Cast of brain in skull

TWO BRAINS
It was once believed that stegosaurs had a second brain which filled a large cavity in the hips. But this is now known to have been a nerve centre, which controlled the hind limbs and the tail.

Large spines for wounding enemies

KENTROSAURU[S]
Six pairs of bony plate[s] ran along the neck an[d] shoulders of *Kentrosaurus*. Behin[d] these plates were three pairs of fl[at] spines and five pairs of long, sharp spine[s]

Tail was held off the ground

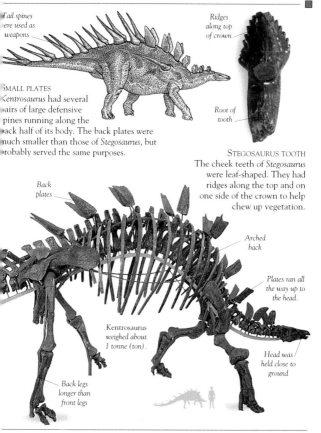

Tail spines
were used as
weapons

Ridges
along top
of crown

SMALL PLATES
Kentrosaurus had several
pairs of large defensive
spines running along the
back half of its body. The back plates were
much smaller than those of *Stegosaurus*, but
probably served the same purposes.

Root of
tooth

STEGOSAURUS TOOTH
The cheek teeth of *Stegosaurus*
were leaf-shaped. They had
ridges along the top and on
one side of the crown to help
chew up vegetation.

Back
plates

Arched
back

Plates ran all
the way up to
the head.

Kentrosaurus
weighed about
1 tonne (ton).

Back legs
longer than
front legs

Head was
held close to
ground

ANKYLOSAURS

PROTECTED BY SPIKES and bony plates, the stocky ankylosaurs were the armoured "tanks" of the dinosaur world. There were two main groups of ankylosaur – the ankylosaurids and the nodosaurids.

SKULL
The triangular skull of *Ankylosaurus* was covered with bony plates. It ended with a horny beak, which it used to crop vegetation.

Ankylosaurids

Many ankylosaurids had spines on their sides as well as bony body scutes (plates). Their most notable feature was a heavy tail club, which they used as a formidable weapon.

EUOPLOCEPHALUS
Euoplocephalus' head was armoured with bony slabs. Its eyelids were bony too, protecting the vulnerable eyes. The stout body and tail club were typical of ankylosaurids.

ANKYLOSAUR FACTS

• The name ankylosaur means "armoured reptile".

• They ranged in length from 1.8 m (6 ft) to 9 m (29½ ft).

• They have been found on all continents, including Antarctica.

• All were covered in bony scutes on their upper side, but were unarmoured on their lower side.

TAIL CLUB

The bony plates were good protection, but the tail club was a very effective weapon. A fearsome tyrannosaurid could be crippled with a well-directed blow to the ankle or shin.

Tyrannosaurus receives a crippling blow

Ankylosaur lashes out at the knee

TAIL CLUB

The tail club was formed by bony plates which were fused together. Powerful tail muscles were used to swing the club. These muscles were anchored by tail vertebrae stiffened by bony tendons.

FOSSILIZED ANKYLOSAURID TAIL CLUB

Euoplocephalus was about 7 m (23 ft) long.

Stiffened, muscular tail

Heavy tail club

Nodosaurids

Armoured with bony plates and dangerous spikes, but lacking the clubbed tail of the ankylosaurids, the nodosaurids were the most primitive of the ankylosaurs. They ranged in length from 1.6 m (5 ft) to 7.6 m (25 ft). Nodosaurid fossils have been found in rocks worldwide.

Gap between jaws for cheek pouch

Plates on top of skull

SHEEP-LIKE SKULL
The pear-shaped skull of *Edmontonia* resembles that of a sheep. It had cheek pouches in which to store food. The top of the skull was reinforced with bony plates for protection.

Crown of tooth with ridged edge

GROUND GRAZER
Edmontonia had small, weak teeth on the sides of its jaws. They were leaf-shaped and flattened – ideal for chopping up leafy vegetation.

Root of tooth

Armour plate

EDMONTONIA
One of the largest of the nodosaurids, *Edmontonia* probably grew to about 7 m (23 ft) in length. Long spikes lined the sides and shoulders, and tough neck plates protected it from tyrannosaurid fangs.

Shoulder spike

Broad head

Wide feet

SAUROPELTA
An armour of spikes, bony cones, and small studs stretched along the back and tail of *Sauropelta*. Its underside was unprotected, so it may have crouched close to the ground when under attack.

Bony cones

Bony studs

Shoulder spikes

Soft, vulnerable underside

Short, stubby legs

ROWS OF PLATES
Sauropelta's cone-shaped plates lay in rows, similar to the bands of armour on a modern giant armadillo.

Stout, strong legs

Armoured tail

Spines on back

Spines on tail

POLACANTHUS
Two rows of spines jutted out of *Polacanthus'* back. There were also two rows of triangular bony scutes along its tail.

ORNITHOPODS

ALL THE ORNITHOPOD dinosaurs were herbivores with horned beaks. Their jaws and leaf-shaped cheek teeth were ideal for chewing vegetation. They were bipedal, although some of them may have foraged for food on all fours. Their feet had three or four toes with hoof-like claws, and their hands had four or five fingers.

Cheek teeth

Tusk-like teeth

HETERODONTOSAURUS
Heterodontosaurus had three different kinds of teeth. These were the front upper teeth, which bit against the toothless lower beak; the scissor-like cheek teeth; and a pair of upper and lower tusk-like teeth.

GROUP LIVING
Hypsilophodon may have moved in herds for protection against predatory theropods. Moving as a large group, they would have been able to warn each other of any danger, giving them a better chance of survival.

Group members looked from side to side for any danger.

Slim, long legs for speed.

Bony tendons

ORNITHOPOD FACTS

• The name ornithopod means "bird foot".

• They ranged in length from 2 m (6½ ft) to 15 m (49 ft).

• Some ornithopods had up to 1,000 cheek teeth.

• They could run at speeds of at least 15 km/h (9 mph).

VERTEBRAE SUPPORT

Ornithopods such as *Iguanodon* had a criss-cross of bony tendons strengthening the vertebrae above the hip and in the back. These bony tendons also stiffened the tail. This helped *Iguanodon* balance as it walked on its two back legs.

Toes ended in flattened hooves

THREE-TOED FEET

The powerful three-toed feet of *Corythosaurus* were built to carry its heavy weight. *Corythosaurus* weighed approximately 4 tonnes (tons) and was about 7.5 m (24 ft) long. It belonged to a group of ornithopods called hadrosaurs.

Hypsilophodon was about 2.3 m (7½ ft) long.

Iguanodonts

These dinosaurs were bipedal herbivores with long toes which ended in hoof-like claws. Their arms were thick and strong, and they may have often walked on all fours, perhaps when foraging for food. Iguanodonts had tall, ridged teeth arranged in a single row, with which they chewed their food before swallowing it. The best-known iguanodonts are *Iguanodon* and *Ouranosaurus*.

Ridges on edge of tooth

Worn-down tooth

WEAR AND TEAR
The *Iguanodon* teeth above are at different stages of wear. The one on the right has been worn down by *Iguanodon*'s diet of tough plants, while the one on the left looks like it has hardly been used.

Iguanodon stabbing a theropod in the neck

STABBING WEAPON
Iguanodon had large, bony thumb spikes. These may have been used as weapons against enemies, such as theropods. *Iguanodon* may have used its thumb spike to stab an attacker through the throat, belly, or eyes.

IGUANODON
The head of *Iguanodon* had a toothless beak for nipping vegetation. Its arms were much shorter than its hind legs, which ended in strong, three-toed feet to support its heavy weight. Its thick tail was very stiff, and was held out almost horizontally.

IGUANODONT FACTS

• The name iguanodont means "iguana tooth".

• They ranged in size from 4 m (13 ft) to 9 m (29½ ft) in length.

• They lived from Late Jurassic through to Late Cretaceous periods.

• An *Iguanodon* shin bone found in 1809 was not identified as belonging to *Iguanodon* until the late 1970s.

Bump on forehead

Ridged teeth

OURANOSAURUS SKULL
Ouranosaurus had a long, duck-like bill, and ridged teeth like those of *Iguanodon*. Its skull was flat-topped with a small bump on its forehead. A special jaw hinge allowed *Ouranosaurus* to chew by sliding the upper jaw outwards against the lower jaw.

Duck-like bill

Iguanodon was about 9 m (29½ ft) long.

Iguanodon weighed about 4.5 tonnes (tons).

Thumb spike

Knee

UPRIGHT POSE
Scientists used to position *Iguanodon*'s skeleton in an upright pose (right). But we now know the stiff tail would not have been able to bend enough to sit on the ground.

Ankle

Upright, kangaroo-like pose is incorrect

Hadrosaurs

These plant eaters are also known as "duckbills", because of their toothless, duck-like bills. Hundreds of self-sharpening teeth arranged in rows lined the sides of the jaws. Hadrosaurs were bipedal. They held their bodies horizontally with their stiffened tails extended for balance. There are two main groups of hadrosaurs: hadrosaurines, with flat-topped skulls, and lambeo-saurines, with hollow head crests.

SECTION OF TIGHTLY PACKED HADROSAUR TEETH

CROSS-SECTION OF HADROSAUR JAW

Upper teeth slid outwards

Lower teeth did not move

CHEWING ACTION

Hadrosaurs chewed food by grating the upper jaw teeth against the lower jaw teeth. The upper jaw was hinged so that when the jaws closed, the upper jaw would slide outwards against the lower jaw.

Bony rods along spine

Deep tail

This Gryposaurus skeleton was found in Alberta, Canada.

HADROSAUR FACTS
- The name hadrosaur means "bulky lizard".
- They ranged in length from 3 m (10 ft) to 15 m (49 ft).
- They are known as the duck-billed dinosaurs because of their long, flat snouts.

GRYPOSAURUS

Like many hadrosaurs, *Gryposaurus* had a trellis of bony rods that stiffened the spine and tail. The deep tail would have been useful when swimming, and shows that hadrosaurs sometimes went into water. But they probably only did this when escaping from enemies.

CORYTHOSAURUS

Although *Corythosaurus* was bipedal, the hoof-shaped claws and padded toes on its hands indicate that it used them a lot for walking. Its diet included the toughest of plants, such as ferns and pine needles. But *Corythosaurus* could easily mash these using its rows of tightly packed teeth.

Hands could hold onto branches

Corythosaurus walked on all fours when feeding on ground-level plants.

Stiff tail was held out horizontally

Hadrosaurines

This group of hadrosaurs had little or no head crest, although some had a bump above the nose which they used for making noises. Some hadrosaurines had bills that curled upwards, forming a spoon shape. They lived in North America, Europe, and Asia during the Late Cretaceous period.

HADROSAUR FAMILY
Maiasaura bred in huge colonies, using the same nesting sites every year. The name *Maiasaura* means "good mother lizard"; *Maiasaura* cared for their young until they could fend for themselves.

Male
Maiasaura
feeding young

Eggs were laid in
a mound made of
earth and plant
material

Female
touches
egg

Large
eyes

Short
snout

JUVENILE MAIASAURA

A juvenile *Maiasaura* differed
in many ways from an adult
Maiasaura. The most
noticeable difference
was the juvenile's
head, which
was much
shorter.

SKELETON OF
JUVENILE
MAIASAURA

*Young Maiasaura were
in constant danger from
predators such as the
tyrannosaurids.*

NOISE POUCH

Edmontosaurus had skin flaps over
its nasal cavities. They normally
lay flat but could inflate,
allowing *Edmontosaurus* to
make bellowing noises.

Wrinkled,
deflated
pouch

*Edmontosaurus may
have made noises to warn
others of danger, attract a
mate, or threaten a rival.*

Pouch inflated
when noise
was made

Lambeosaurines

Large bony head crests were a distinctive feature of these hadrosaurs. Powerful limbs supported a heavy body, and the downward-curving lower jaw had a broad, blunt beak. They lived around the same time as the hadrosaurines, and their remains have been found in North America and Asia.

HYPACROSAURUS SKULL

Hollow head crest

Wide "duckbill" snout

Hundreds of tightly packed teeth

Hypacrosaurus was 9 m (29½ ft) long

SOUND MAKERS
The head crest of *Hypacrosaurus* was made of bones which grew up from the nose. Hadrosaurs probably used their hollow crests to amplify the sound of their calls, although the crests may also have improved their sense of smell.

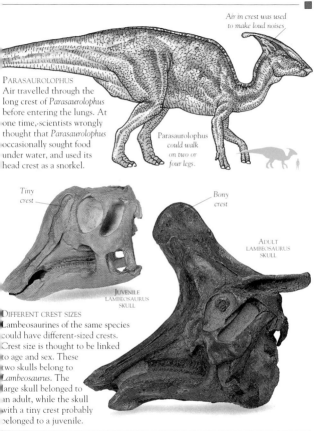

Air in crest was used
to make loud noises

PARASAUROLOPHUS
Air travelled through the
long crest of *Parasaurolophus*
before entering the lungs. At
one time, scientists wrongly
thought that *Parasaurolophus*
occasionally sought food
under water, and used its
head crest as a snorkel.

*Parasaurolophus
could walk
on two or
four legs.*

Tiny
crest

Bony
crest

ADULT
LAMBEOSAURUS
SKULL

JUVENILE
LAMBEOSAURUS
SKULL

DIFFERENT CREST SIZES
Lambeosaurines of the same species
could have different-sized crests.
Crest size is thought to be linked
to age and sex. These
two skulls belong to
Lambeosaurus. The
large skull belonged to
an adult, while the skull
with a tiny crest probably
belonged to a juvenile.

PACHYCEPHALOSAURS

THE THICK, DOMED skulls of pachycephalosaurs earned them the name "bone-headed dinosaurs". Rival males used to bash their heads together, their brains protected by the thick bone. Pachycephalosaurs probably had a good sense of smell, which would have allowed them to detect nearby predators and escape before the predators got too close.

HORN CLUSTER
Stygimoloch had a cluster of horns behind its dome. But the horns were probably just for show, rather than of practical use.

LOTS OF NODULES
Prenocephale's head had a well-developed solid dome and small nodules on the back of the skull.

PACHYCEPHALOSAUR FACTS

• The name pachycephalosaur means "thick-headed lizard".

• They ranged in length from 90 cm (3 ft) to 4.6 m (15 ft).

• Diet included fruits, leaves, and insects.

STEGOCERAS
Goat-sized *Stegoceras* was about 2.4 m (8 ft) long. Several *Stegoceras* skulls have been found with domes of various thicknesses. The domes of juveniles were not as thick or high as those of adults, especially adult males.

Prenocephale run towards each other at full tilt

HEAD BANGERS
Male pachycephalosaurs may have had head-butting bouts when fighting over territory and females, the way that mountain goats do today.

Knobs on nose

THICK SKULL
The solid dome of *Pachycephalosaurus* could be as thick as 23 cm (9 in). Small knobs and spikes fringed the dome and decorated the small nose.

The name Stegoceras means "horny roof".

Bony tendons held the back vertebrae stiffly together.

STIFF BACK
Stegoceras, like all pachycephalosaurs, was bipedal, but it was unlikely to have been fast on its feet. It kept its back level, with the front of its body balanced by the stiffened heavy tail.

Predators of Stegoceras included Tyrannosaurus rex.

Short arms and small hands

CERATOPSIANS

HORNS, BONY FRILLS, and a
parrot-like beak were the trademarks of the ceratopsians. They
were all quadrupedal herbivores,
and many ceratopsians lived in great
herds. Most ceratopsians can be divided
into two groups. One group had short neck frills, the
other had long neck frills. The ceratopsians were
among the last dinosaurs to
become extinct.

PSITTACOSAURUS
SKULL

Psittacosaurus
may have moved
on all fours
when foraging.

PSITTACOSAURUS
This dinosaur was a 2-m- (6½-ft-)
long bipedal ancestor of the
ceratopsians. It had a
parrot-like beak
and a very small
neck frill, but
lacked the horns of
other ceratopsians.

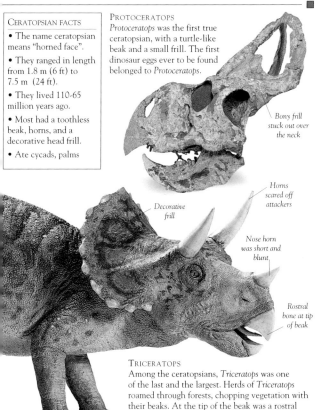

CERATOPSIAN FACTS

• The name ceratopsian means "horned face".

• They ranged in length from 1.8 m (6 ft) to 7.5 m (24 ft).

• They lived 110-65 million years ago.

• Most had a toothless beak, horns, and a decorative head frill.

• Ate cycads, palms

PROTOCERATOPS

Protoceratops was the first true ceratopsian, with a turtle-like beak and a small frill. The first dinosaur eggs ever to be found belonged to *Protoceratops*.

Bony frill stuck out over the neck

Decorative frill

Horns scared off attackers

Nose horn was short and blunt

Rostral bone at tip of beak

TRICERATOPS

Among the ceratopsians, *Triceratops* was one of the last and the largest. Herds of *Triceratops* roamed through forests, chopping vegetation with their beaks. At the tip of the beak was a rostral bone, which was common to all ceratopsians.

Short-frilled ceratopsians

The group of ceratopsians with short frills also had long nose horns and short brow horns. *Styracosaurus* had the most dramatic frill, with long horns growing out from its edge. The discovery of five young near an adult *Brachyceratops* indicates that these ceratopsians looked after their young. It is likely that when a herd was in danger from predators, the males protected the young and the females.

STYRACOSAURUS
SKULL

Long
nose
horn

STYRACOSAURUS
Six long spikes edged the frill of *Styracosaurus*. It had a lethal horn on its nose that was 60 cm (2 ft) long and 15 cm (6 in) thick. The horns above the eyes, however, were only stumps. It was possibly a good runner, capable of speeds of up to 32 km/h (20 mph).

Horns on
edge of
frill

Nose
horn

FOSSIL BEAK
Ceratopsian dinosaurs had beaks that were ideal for slicing through twigs and tough plants. Each beak had a horny covering which was attached to the grooves and pits on the surface.

Horny covering was attached to grooves on surface

Bony hook

Stumps along edge of frill

CENTROSAURUS
The horn on the nose of *Centrosaurus'* curved forwards rather than backwards like most other ceratopsians. The short frill had small stumps along the edge, as well as a pair of long central hooks which projected forwards.

A rhinocerous has two horns on its nose.

SIMILAR BODIES
Rhinoceroses resemble ceratopsians with their stocky bodies and facial horns. A charging rhinoceros reaches speeds of up to 45 km/h (28 mph), and it is thought that ceratopsians such as *Centrosaurus* could run at least as fast.

Long-frilled ceratopsians

The frill of long-frilled ceratopsians extended back to, or over, the shoulders. Sometimes the bony frill was armed with short spikes, and there were often holes in the frill to lighten the load. The snout had a short horn and there were long brow horns – the opposite of the short-frilled ceratopsians.

Horn was made of solid bone

Brow horn

FOSSIL HORN
This fossil is the core of the brow horn of *Triceratops*. In life it would have been sheathed in horn.

IDEAL SKULL
Triceratops had a solid bony frill, a short nose horn, and two 1-m- (3-ft-) long brow horns. The parrot-like beak and scissor-like teeth were ideal for *Triceratops'* vegetarian diet.

Beak was used to crop vegetation

Sharp teeth cut up leaves

TOROSAURUS
The skull of *Torosaurus*, from the tip of the snout to the back of the frill, was 2.6 m (8½ ft) long – about the size of a small car. *Torosaurus'* head was bigger than that of any other known land animal.

Two large holes in the frill bone reduced its weight.

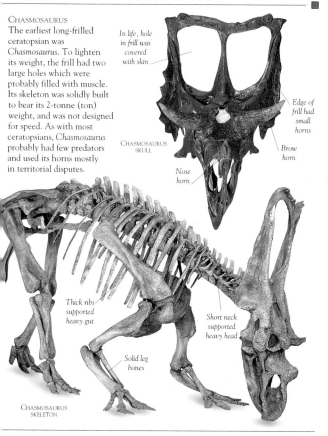

CHASMOSAURUS

The earliest long-frilled ceratopsian was *Chasmosaurus*. To lighten its weight, the frill had two large holes which were probably filled with muscle. Its skeleton was solidly built to bear its 2-tonne (ton) weight, and was not designed for speed. As with most ceratopsians, *Chasmosaurus* probably had few predators and used its horns mostly in territorial disputes.

In life, hole in frill was covered with skin

Edge of frill had small horns

Brow horn

CHASMOSAURUS SKULL

Nose horn

Thick ribs supported heavy gut

Short neck supported heavy head

Solid leg bones

CHASMOSAURUS SKELETON

REPTILES OF THE
SEA AND AIR

ABOUT SEA AND AIR REPTILES

WHILE THE DINOSAURS lived on land, other reptiles lived in the sea and flew in the air. The sea reptiles, such as the ichthyosaurs and plesiosaurs needed to breathe air and would have surfaced frequently to fill their lungs. The flying reptiles, called pterosaurs, included the largest ever flying animals. There were two groups of pterosaur – rhamphorhynchoids and pterodactyloids.

Wing made of skin

Clawed foot

Furry body

Short tail

Sharp teeth in long beak

Clawed fingers

Pterodactylus was a small pterosaur with a wingspan of only 50 cm (20 in).

FUR FOR WARMTH
Pterodactylus was a pterodactyloid from the Jurassic period. Some *Pterodactylus* fossils showed small fur-like impressions around the body. This suggests that pterosaurs may have been warm blooded and would have used fur to keep themselves warm

Tapered
tail

Long skull

Large
flipper

PELONEUSTES
Fish, shellfish, and smaller
sea reptiles formed the diet of the
sea predator *Peloneustes*. Its barrel-
shaped body had large flippers for
speeding through the water.

ICHTHYOSAURUS
Ichthyosaurs, such as
Ichthyosaurus, were similar
in shape to modern
dolphins. Like dolphins,
hthyosaurs would have
been fast swimmers
ue to their stream-
lined shape.

Dolphins
are the
crobats of
the sea.

DOLPHINS
Dolphins steer with
their fins as they
chase fish to eat
at speeds of up to
50 km/h (31 mph).
It is possible that
ichthyosaurs swam as
fast as dolphins, and
lived in a similar manner.

Dolphins are
mammals,
but they have
no hair.

RARE FOSSILS
Pterosaur fossils
are rare because they had
light, fragile bones. The
lightness of the bones was
important to allow flight.

Ichthyosaurus
was about 2 m
(6½ ft) long.

REPTILES AT SEA

THE SEA REPTILES evolved from land reptiles which adapted to life in the water. The legs and feet shortened and widened to become paddles, and the body became streamlined for faster movement through water. These reptiles were carnivores, preying on other sea creatures as well as each other.

MODIFIED PADDLE
The plesiosaur *Cryptoclidus* was 4 m (13 ft) long and had four paddles which were each about 1 m (3 ft) long. It swam by flexing these powerful paddles up and down, "flying" through the water in the way that penguins do today.

Each paddle had five elongated toes.

Large and sharp teeth

Curved and conical teeth

FLEXIBLE JAWS
Masosaurus was a giant marine lizard which lived in Late Cretaceous shallow coastal waters. The skull and lower jaw bones had flexible joints and curved, piercing teeth. This would enable *Masosaurus* to give a wide and lethal bite.

Powerful, flexible paddles propelled Pliosaurus *through the water.*

All plesiosaurs had very long necks and small heads.

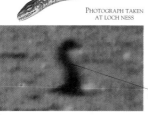

PHOTOGRAPH TAKEN AT LOCH NESS

Could this be the Loch Ness Monster?

MYSTERIOUS MONSTER

Many people claim to have seen a large creature swimming in Loch Ness in Scotland. This animal, known as the Loch Ness Monster, has been described as a living relative of the plesiosaurs.

MURAENOSAURUS

Air-filled lungs meant that the plesiosaur *Muraenosaurus* would have found it easier to float than to dive underwater. To combat this, it probably swallowed pebbles to weigh itself down, the way that crocodiles do today.

Scaly skin

Tail flipper

The skin would have been scaly, like the reptiles on land.

PLIOSAURUS

One of the fiercest predators of its time, *Pliosaurus* hunted in the seas of the Jurassic period 150 million years ago. It was about 7 m (23 ft) long and fed on fish and smaller sea reptiles. Like all pliosaurs, *Pliosaurus* had a short neck, a large head, and a barrel-shaped body. It also had strong jaws and large, sharp teeth with which it could crush and kill prey.

SEA REPTILE FACTS

• They breathed air.

• They were carnivores.

• The turtles are the only sea reptiles still living.

• Ichthyosaurs bore live young; all other reptiles laid eggs.

More reptiles at sea

Plesiosaurs, pliosaurs, and turtles probably hauled themselves onto beaches to lay eggs, the way modern turtles do. Ichthyosaurs did not leave the water since they were fully adapted to life at sea and gave birth to live young. By the time the dinosaurs died out, all sea reptiles, apart from the turtles, had become extinct, too. The reason for this is as mysterious as the disappearance of the dinosaurs.

Fossil shell of the 30-cm- (12-in-) long turtle Cimochelys

FOSSIL SHELLS
Fossilized ancient turtle shells show that these turtles had the same bony armour as modern turtles.

Archelon was 6 m (20 ft) long.

ARCHELON
Like its descendants, the modern turtles, *Archelon* may have returned to the same beaches every year to lay eggs. Both the adult *Archelon* and its eggs would have been vulnerable to predatory dinosaurs of that time.

EYE PROTECTION
Ichthyosaurs were carnivores with long beaks and pointed teeth. A bony ring surrounded each eye. These rings may have protected the eyes from high water pressure when diving to great depths.

Bony ring around eye

Long jaw

Sharp teeth

Large eye socket

Very thin, tooth-lined snout

STENOPTERYGIUS
Some fossilized adult ichthyosaur skeletons contain the skeletons of unborn young. This fossil of *Stenopterygius* is so well preserved it is possible to see the outline of the smooth body shape left by the skin.

Skin impression

Tail was moved from side to side for propulsion and steering

Shonisaurus was the largest ichthyosaur.

SHONISAURUS
Giant *Shonisaurus* was 15 m (49 ft) long. Large groups of *Shonisaurus* skeletons have been found in North America. This suggests that they were prone to mysterious mass beachings (being stranded on a beach and dying), similar to present-day whales.

REPTILES IN THE AIR

THE PTEROSAURS were the first ever flying vertebrates (animals with a backbone). Their wings were a thin membrane of muscles and elastic fibres covered with skin. The rhamphorhynchoid group of pterosaurs had long tails and short heads with sharp teeth. They first appeared in the Triassic period and became extinct at the end of the Jurassic period.

Stiff tail may have been used for steering when flying

RHAMPHORHYNCHUS
Rhamphorhynchus, a rhamphorhynchoid, had a special beak for trawling the water surface to catch fish while flying. The jaws were armed with large, forward-pointing spike teeth behind a toothless beak.

Large skull

Long tail typical of rhampho-rhynchoids

FOSSIL
This fossil skeleton of the rhamphorhynchoid *Dimorphodon* shows the fine bones and the skull which was very large compared to the body.

Pointed teeth

SORDES
A thick coat of insulating "hair" covered Sordes' body. But its hairs were not like the hairs of a mammal – they probably developed from reptile scales, like the feathers of a bird.

Elongated fourth finger supporting wing

Dimorphodon lived 190 million years ago and was one of the first pterosaurs.

Wing covered with skin

Clawed fingers

Large, deep snout with sharp teeth

DIMORPHODON
Like all pterosaurs, the wings of Dimorphodon were supported by an elongated fourth finger. The other three fingers on Dimorphodon's hands were large and clawed and may have been used for climbing rocks and cliffs.

Dimorphodon had a wingspan of 1.4 m (4½ ft).

The legs were powerful, which suggests that they were used for walking and running.

More reptiles in the air

The pterodactyloid group of pterosaurs included the largest animals ever to take to the air. Pterodactyloids had long heads, long necks, and short tails. The head had a large crest, which may have acted as a counterbalance to the long beak. Some pterodactyloids had specialized teeth, such as *Pterodaustro*, whose teeth were bristle-like for filtering food. Most pterodactyloids would have skimmed the water surface for fish with their long jaws.

PTERANODON
The head of *Pteranodon* was 1.8 m (6 ft) long from the tip of its beak to the back of its crest. Some *Pteranodons* lacked a crest, which may have been a difference between the sexes.

Head crest

Short tail

Clawed feet

Pointed beak

Long, curved neck

Toothless beak

WING FINGER
This is a fossilized bone from *Pteranodon's* elongated wing finger. The wing finger consisted of long, thin, and very ligh bones which extended to the tip of the wing. *Pteranodon* was one of the largest pterosaurs, with a wingspan of 7 m (23 ft).

Criorhynchus had a wingspan of 5 m (16½ ft).

Upright crest on upper jaw

Quetzalcoatlus had a wingspan of 12 m (39½ ft).

ROUND CREST
The most distinctive feature of *Criorhynchus* was the rounded crest at the front of the upper jaw. This crest probably helped *Criorhynchus* to stabilize its head in the water while fishing.

LARGEST FLYER
Quetzalcoatlus was the largest flying creature ever. It had a long, thin beak which it may have used to probe for molluscs in the mud. It may also have fed on the carcasses of dead animals, like vultures do today.

Clawed fingers

Delicate skull

Upper arm bone

Long, curved neck

Wing finger

FINE FOSSIL
Pterodactylus was an agile flyer which probably fed on insects. This fossil skeleton embedded in limestone shows *Pterodactylus'* delicate skull and fine bones.

Quetzalcoatlus may have weighed about 86 kg (190 lb).

REFERENCE
SECTION

DINOSAUR DISCOVERERS

PEOPLE HAVE probably found dinosaur fossils for thousands of years. But it was not until 1841 that scientists first identified the dinosaur group. There have been many well-known dinosaur hunters, made famous because of the dinosaurs they have discovered.

SIR RICHARD OWEN (1804-92) was a famous British anatomist. He coined the name "dinosaur", which means "terrible lizard".

WHAT HE DISCOVERED
Owen worked at the Natural History Museum in London, where he studied fossils found in Europe. He not only realized that some fossils were reptiles, but were unknown types of giant reptiles. He concluded that they must have belonged to a group of extinct animals, and named this group dinosaurs.

DR. GIDEON MANTELL (1790-1852) was a medical doctor from Sussex in England. He was also a keen fossil hunter. He spent much of his early life collecting fossils in the hills near where he lived. But it was one fossil find which put his name in the history books.

WHAT HE DISCOVERED
In 1820, Gideon Mantell and his wife, Mary Ann, found some large teeth and bones in some gravel near a stone quarry. They belonged to an unknown, iguana-like animal. In 1825 he named it *Iguanodon*, although he did not realize at the time that it was a dinosaur.

DEAN WILLIAM BUCKLAND (1784-1856) was the first professor of geology at Oxford University in England. He was fascinated by fossils from an early age.

WHAT HE DISCOVERED
In 1824, a large jawbone with a giant tooth was found near Oxford. Buckland recognized it as belonging to a previously unknown giant reptile. This reptile was named *Megalosaurus*, which means "big lizard", and was the first dinosaur to be named. Like Mantell, Buckland did not know that *Megalosaurus* was a dinosaur.

JOHN BELL HATCHER (1861-1904) was a fossil collector for Othniel Marsh. Hatcher is recognized as one of the greatest collectors of dinosaurs in the history of American palaeontology.

WHAT HE DISCOVERED
In 1888, Hatcher found part of a huge skull with horns beside the Judith River in Montana. It turned out to be a *Triceratops* skull, and was the first fossil of this dinosaur to be discovered. It was also the first of the horned dinosaurs to be found, which introduced a new dinosaur variety to palaeontologists.

EDWARD DRINKER COPE (1840-97) was an American from Philadelphia. He was a scientific genius, and dinosaurs were just one area on which he was an expert.

WHAT HE DISCOVERED
Cope started his scientific career after the American Civil War. He travelled with fellow scientist Othaniel Marsh on many of his early trips. They eventually became fierce rivals. Among his many finds, Cope discovered several primitive Triassic dinosaurs from New Mexico.

OTHNIEL CHARLES MARSH (1831-99) was an American palaeontologist born in New York. Along with E.D. Cope, Marsh was one of the great pioneers of dinosaur fossil hunting in the United States.

WHAT HE DISCOVERED
Marsh discovered many dinosaur fossil sites in the United States. The most famous were Como Bluff in Wyoming and several sites in Colorado. His intense rivalry with Edward Drinker Cope was nicknamed the "Bone Wars".

EBERHARD FRAAS (1862-1915) was a German palaeontologist. He went on long expeditions to Africa in his search for dinosaurs fossils.

WHAT HE DISCOVERED
In 1907, Fraas was told of some dinosaur bones in a site in Tanzania, Africa. Fraas led an expedition set up to explore the site and, in 1909-12, the first fine specimens of *Kentrosaurus*, *Elaphrosaurus*, *Barosaurus*, and *Brachiosaurus* were discovered there. The *Brachiosaurus* skeleton Fraas discovered is now in a museum in Berlin, and is the largest mounted skeleton in the world.

GEORGE F. STERNBERG (1883-1969) was an American palaeontologist who started collecting fossils at the age of six. He continued to work on fossils for the next 66 years.

WHAT HE DISCOVERED
George F. Sternberg made his most important dinosaur discovery in 1908: he was the first person to find an impression of dinosaur skin, which belonged to *Anatosaurus*. Sternberg made many other amazing discoveries, including the first fossil of *Edmontosaurus*.

EDWIN COLBERT (b.1905) is an American palaeontologist and an expert in Triassic dinosaurs. He was the first to find dinosaur fossils in Antarctica. He has written several books about the history of dinosaurs.

WHAT HE DISCOVERED
Colbert found the first complete *Coelophysis* skeletons in New Mexico, U.S.A in 1947. Some skeletons held the bones of young *Coelophysis* in the rib cage. This indicated that *Coelophysis* may have been a cannibal.

ANDREW CARNEGIE (1835-1919) was originally from Scotland. He emigrated with his family to the United States at the age of 11. He made his fortune in the steel industry in Pittsburgh.

WHAT HE DISCOVERED
Carnegie set up the Carnegie Museum in Pittsburgh. He sent fossil hunters on long expeditions to find dinosaurs for his museum. They discovered two complete skeletons of *Diplodocus*. A replica of one of the skeletons stands in the Natural History Museum in London.

ROY CHAPMAN ANDREWS (1884-1960) led the first American expedition to the Gobi Desert in Mongolia in 1922. Andrews went with a team from the American Museum of Natural History (AMNH).

WHAT HE DISCOVERED
Andrews and his team discovered many new dinosaurs in the Gobi Desert. Among them were *Protoceratops*, *Velociraptor*, and *Oviraptor*. But the most significant find was some fossilized *Protoceratops* eggs – the first dinosaur eggs to be discovered.

EARL DOUGLASS (1862-1931) was an American from Utah. He worked at the Carnegie Museum in Pittsburgh. Andrew Carnegie, who founded the museum, wanted to exhibit skeletons of the giant dinosaurs.

WHAT HE DISCOVERED
In 1909 Douglass was sent by Andrew Carnegie to hunt for fossils in Utah. Douglass' discoveries included *Diplodocus* and *Apatosaurus*. The site where these dinosaurs were found was turned into the Dinosaur National Park, which still exists today.

BARNUM BROWN (1873-1963), an American, was hired by the American Museum of Natural History in New York because of his skill in finding dinosaur skeletons.

WHAT HE DISCOVERED
Barnum Brown's expertise in fossil hunting earned him the nickname "Mr. Bones". He found the first *Tyrannosaurus rex* fossils, and named *Ankylosaurus* and *Corythosaurus*. The AMNH houses the world's greatest display of Cretaceous dinosaurs as a result of Brown's collecting.

JIM JENSON (b.1910) is a self-taught palaeontologist. He was the curator of the Vertebrate Palaeontology Research Laboratory at Brigham Young University in Utah, U.S.A.

WHAT HE DISCOVERED
Jenson has discovered some of the largest dinosaurs. In 1972, he found a partial skeleton of a sauropod. He named it *Supersaurus*. *Supersaurus'* height is estimated to be 16.5 m (54 ft). In 1979 he found a partial skeleton of another new sauropod. He named it *Ultrasaurus*, and it is thought to be even bigger than *Supersaurus*.

BILL WALKER (b. 1928) is a British quarry-worker who is also an amateur fossil collector. In 1982, he made an important dinosaur discovery when exploring a muddy clay pit in Surrey, England.

WHAT HE DISCOVERED
Walker found a huge claw, which broke into pieces when he held it. He took it to the British Museum in London, which organized an excavation to recover more of the creature. It turned out to be a new dinosaur, which was named *Baryonyx walkeri*, in honour of Walker.

REPTILES CLASSIFIED

ALL LIVING THINGS are classified into different groups, according to their common features. In the animal kingdom, vertebrates form a huge group. All vertebrates have a backbone – that is their common feature. This chart shows how reptiles, including the dinosaurs, fit into the vertebrate group.

FISH

FISHES AND SHARKS

AMPHIBIANS

AMPHIBI

VERTEBRATES

REPTILES

VERTEBRATES
All vertebrates have an internal skeleton, which supports their body. This distinguishes them from animals without an internal skeleton, such as insects, which are called invertebrates.

MAMMALS

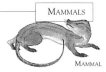

MAMMAL

RECONSTRUCTION OF "LIZZIE"

"LIZZIE"
A fossil reptile found in Scotland is the oldest reptile we know of. The 330-million-year-old reptile, named "Lizzie" by its discoverer, was 30 cm (1 ft) long. Its skin was scaly and waterproof, like the skin of modern reptiles.

FOUR GROUPS
There are four main groups of vertebrate – fishes, amphibians, reptiles, and mammals. Each of these groups have hundreds, or even thousands, of subgroups.

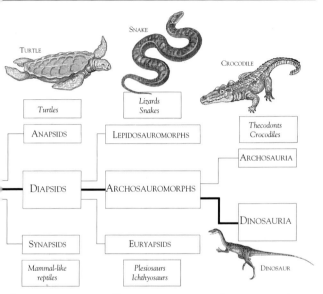

TURTLE

SNAKE

CROCODILE

Turtles

Lizards
Snakes

Thecodonts
Crocodiles

ANAPSIDS

LEPIDOSAUROMORPHS

ARCHOSAURIA

DIAPSIDS

ARCHOSAUROMORPHS

DINOSAURIA

SYNAPSIDS

EURYAPSIDS

Mammal-like
reptiles

Plesiosaurs
Ichthyosaurs

DINOSAUR

REPTILE GROUPS
The reptile group is
divided into three
subgroups. These three
divisions are based on
the number of openings
in the skull behind the
eye sockets. The
anapsids have no
openings; the synsapsids
have one, and the
diapsids have two.

DIAPSIDS
The diapsids are further
divided into three
groups. These are:
lepidosauromorphs,
which include lizards
and snakes; archosauro-
morphs, which include
dinosaurs and crocodiles;
and eurapsids, which
include the plesiosaurs
and the ichthyosaurs.

ARCHOSAUROMORPHS
The dinosaurs are in
this group, as well as
the thecodonts, which
are thought to be the
ancestors of the
dinosaurs. Other
members of the
archosauromorph
group include
pterosaurs, crocodiles,
and birds.

Dinosaurs classified

The classification of dinosaurs is controversial and is continually being revised. In this chart, dinosaurs are subdivided into three main groups – Herrerasauria (early predatory dinosaurs), Saurischia, and Ornithischia. Birds (Aves) are now considered to be dinosaurs because primitive birds, such as *Archaeopteryx*, shared many features in common with theropods.

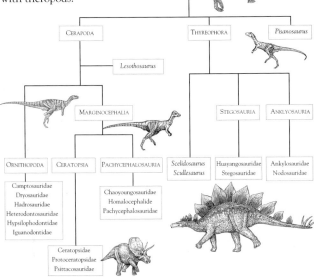

ORNITHISCHIA

CERAPODA | THYREOPHORA | *Pisanosaurus*

Lesothosaurus

MARGINOCEPHALIA | STEGOSAURIA | ANKLYOSAURIA

ORNITHOPODA | CERATOPSIA | PACHYCEPHALOSAURIA | | |

ORNITHOPODA	PACHYCEPHALOSAURIA	STEGOSAURIA	ANKLYOSAURIA
Camptosauridae		*Scelidosaurus*	Ankylosauridae
Dryosauridae	Chaoyoungosauridae	*Scullesaurus*	Nodosauridae
Hadrosauridae	Homalocephalide	Huayangosauridae	
Heterodontosauridae	Pachycephalosauridae	Stegosauridae	
Hypsilophodontidae			
Iguanodontidae			

Ceratopsidae
Protoceratopsidae
Psittacosauridae

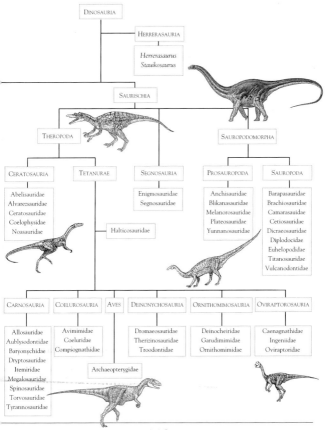

DINOSAURIA

HERRERASAURIA

Herrerasaurus
Staurikosaurus

SAURISCHIA

THEROPODA

SAUROPODOMORPHA

CERATOSAURIA

Abelisauridae
Alvarezsauridae
Ceratosauridae
Coelophysidae
Noasauridae

TETANURAE

Halticosauridae

SEGNOSAURIA

Enigmosauridae
Segnosauridae

PROSAUROPODA

Anchisauridae
Blikanasauridae
Melanorosauridae
Plateosauridae
Yunnanosauridae

SAUROPODA

Barapasauridae
Brachiosauridae
Camarasauridae
Cetiosauridae
Dicraeosauridae
Diplodocidae
Euhelopodidae
Titanosauridae
Vulcanodontidae

CARNOSAURIA

Allosauridae
Aublysodontidae
Baryonychidae
Dryptosauridae
Itemiridae
Megalosauridae
Spinosauridae
Torvosauridae
Tyrannosauridae

COELUROSAURIA

Avimimidae
Coeluridae
Compsognathidae

AVES

Archaeopterygidae

DEINONYCHOSAURIA

Dromaeosauridae
Therizinosauridae
Troodontidae

ORNITHOMIMOSAURIA

Deinocheiridae
Garudimimidae
Ornithomimidae

OVIRAPTOROSAURIA

Caenagnathidae
Ingeniidae
Oviraptoridae

RECORDS AND MYTHS

AS SCIENCE HAS ADVANCED, so has our understanding of dinosaurs. With almost every new discovery, we learn more about these giant reptiles. The early dinosaur experts had beliefs about dinosaurs which we now know to be incorrect. The largest, smallest, fastest, most intelligent, or the least intelligent dinosaur also changes as our knowledge increases.

DINOSAUR RECORDS

• The smallest dinosaur ever found was called *Mussaurus*. It was only 20 cm (8 in) long, but the single skeleton found may have been a hatchling. The smallest adult dinosaur we know of was *Compsognathus*, which was about the size of a chicken.

• *Dromiceiomimus* may have been the fastest of the dinosaurs, running at speeds of over 70 km/h (43 mph).

• The sauropod *Mamenchisaurus* had the longest neck of any dinosaur. The length of the neck was around 14 m (46 ft).

• *Tyrannosaurus rex* was the largest meat-eating dinosaur that ever lived. It was about 14 m (46 ft) long, and 6 m (18 ft) high. Its powerful jaws had teeth as long as 18 cm (7 in).

• The biggest dinosaur that we know of was the sauropod *Seismosaurus*. It was about 40 m (131 ft) long and weighed about 51 tonnes (tons).

• The herbivorous hadrosaurs had about 960 teeth – more than any other dinosaur. That was about 480 tightly packed teeth in each jaw.

• *Troodon* had the largest brain in proportion to its size of any dinosaur.

• *Stegosaurus* had the smallest brain in proportion to its size.

• *Barosaurus* had the longest tail of all the dinosaurs, at over 13 m (43 ft) in length.

DINOSAUR MYTHS

• In 1822, Gideon Mantell made a reconstruction of *Iguanodon*, based on the few bones he had found. He had only one thumb spike, which he thought belonged to *Iguanodon*'s nose. This was similar to the nose spike of an iguana lizard, after which *Iguanodon* was named. It was not until the discovery of several skeletons in the late 1800s that scientists realized this mistake.

• In China, the word "konglong" means both "dinosaur" and "terrible dragon". The Chinese have been collecting dinosaur fossils for 2,000 years. Since the third century A.D., and perhaps before then, the Chinese believed that dinosaur bones were actually the remains of dragons.

• Many films and books portray dinosaurs and humans as living at the same time. In fact, dinosaurs became extinct over 60 million years before the first humans appeared.

• It used to be thought that all dinosaurs dragged their tails on the ground, like modern lizards. Some sauropods probably did, but most dinosaurs had stiffened tails, which they held horizontally off the ground.

• *Hypsilophodon* was once thought to have lived in trees. It was believed that their long tails helped them to balance in the branches, and their sharp claws were used for clinging. We now know their fingers and toes were not designed for gripping branches.

• Many people think that dinosaurs were all huge and cumbersome. But the vast majority were only about as big as an elephant, and some were as small as a chicken. Most were very agile, too.

• It was thought that *Brachiosaurus* lived in water because of the high position of its nostrils. But the great water pressures at depth would not have allowed it to breathe.

• *Iguanodon* was the first dinosaur to be reconstructed. At first it was shown as a slow, sprawling lizard, dragging a fat belly on the ground. We now know that *Iguanodon* was actually bipedal and much slimmer.

DIGGING UP DINOSAURS

MANY IMPORTANT dinosaur discoveries are made by
professional and amateur collectors. Once discovered,
fossil bones should be removed only by experienced
professionals, because the bones are often fragile. The
method of removing the bones depends on a number
of factors, but generally follows a similar procedure.

1 SITE
Once a dinosaur site has been
uncovered, the fossil bones have to be
excavated (dug up). This delicate
operation is carried out using special tools.

2 EXCAVATION
Hammers, chisels, and picks are used
to remove most of the matrix (earth and
stone material surrounding the bones).

3 EXPOSING THE BONES
Whenever possible, the matrix is
removed close to the bone. This is done
with great care so as to not damage the
bone. The bones are exposed to reveal
their full size so that no fragment will
be left behind when removed.

5 JACKET ON OTHER SIDE
Once the exposed part of the bone has been coated, the rest of the bone, including some of the matrix, can be dug out of the ground. It is then covered with a plaster and burlap jacket.

4 PLASTER JACKET
The exposed part of the bones are coated with glue and covered with a jacket of plaster and burlap (a type of canvas). This will protect the bones as they travel from the site to a museum, where they can be studied in more detail.

6 REMOVAL FROM SITE
The jacketed bones are sometimes so big and heavy that a crane is needed to lift them onto a truck.

Resources

ARGENTINA

Museum of La Plata University
La Plata

AUSTRALIA

Queensland Museum
Gregory Terrace
Fortitude Valley
Queensland 4006

Museum of Victoria
328 Swanston Street
Melbourne
Victoria 3000

Australian Museum
College Street
Sydney
New South Wales 2000

AUSTRIA

Natural History Museum
1 Marcia-Theresien-Platz
Vienna

BELGIUM

Royal Institute of Natural Sciences
Rue Vautier 29
B-1040 Brussels

CANADA

Canadian Museum of Nature
National Museum of Canada
240 McLeod Avenue
Ottawa
Ontario K1A 0MB

Royal Ontario Museum
100 Queen's Park
Toronto
Ontario M5S 2C

INDIA

Geology Museum
Indian Statistical Institute
Calcutta

ITALY

Municipal Museum of Natural History
S. Croce 1730
30125 Venice

JAPAN

National Science Museum
Tokyo

MEXICO

Natural History Museum
Mexico City

NEW ZEALAND

Canterbury Museum
Rolleston Avenue
Christchurch 1

POLAND

Dinosaur Park
Chorzow, Silesia
Institute of Palaeobiology
Al Zwirki I Wigury 93
02-089 Warsaw

RUSSIA

Palaeontological Institute
Academy of Science
Moscow 117321

Central Geological and Prospecting Museum
St Petersburg

SOUTH AFRICA

South African Museum
Cape Town

Bernard Price Institute
for Palaeontological
Research
University of
Witwatersrand
Jan Smuts Avenue
Johannesburg 2001

SPAIN

**Natural Science
Museum**
Madrid

SWEDEN

**Palaeontological
Museum**
Uppsala University
751 05 Uppsala

UNITED KINGDOM

Ulster Museum
Botanic Gardens
Belfast BT9 5AB

Birmingham Museum
Chamberlain Square
Birmingham B3 3DH

Museum of Geology
Cambridge University
Downing Street
Cambridge CB2 3EQ

**National Museum of
Wales**
Cathays Park
Cardiff CF1 3NP

The Dinosaur Museum
Icen Way
Dorchester
Dorset DT1 1EW

**National Museums of
Scotland**
Chambers Street
Edinburgh EH1 1JF

Hunterian Museum
University of Glasgow
University Avenue
Glasgow G12 8QQ

Leicestershire Museums
96 New Walk
Leicester LE1 6TD

**British Museum
(Natural History)**
Cromwell Road
London SW7 5BD

Crystal Palace Park
Sydenham
London SE20

Maidstone Museum
Faiths Street
Maidstone
Kent ME14 1LH

University Museum
Parks Road
Oxford OX1 3PW

Museum of Isle of Wight
Sandown Library
High Street
Sandown
Isle of Wight PO35 8AF

UNITED STATES

**American Museum of
Natural History**
Central Park West/
79th Street
New York NY 10024

**Carnegie Museum of
Natural History**
4400 Forbes Avenue
Pittsburgh
Pennsylvania 15213

**Field Museum of
Natural History**
Roosevelt Road at Lake
Shore Drive
Chicago
Illinois 60605

**Peabody Museum of
Natural History**
Yale University
170 Whitney Avenue
New Haven
Connecticut 06511

Pronunciation guide

ALBERTOSAURUS
(al-BERT-oh-SORE-us)

ALLOSAURUS
(al-oh-SORE-us)

ANCHISAURUS
(AN-ki-SORE-us)

ANKYLOSAURUS
(an-KIE-loh-SORE-us)

APATOSAURUS
(ah-PAT-oh-SORE-us)

ARCHAEOPTERYX
(ark-ee-OP-ter-iks)

BAROSAURUS
(bar-oh-SORE-us)

BARYONYX
(bar-ee-ON-iks)

BRACHIOSAURUS
(brak-ee-oh-SORE-us)

CARNOTAURUS
(kar-noh-TOR-us)

CENTROSAURUS
(SEN-troh-SORE-us)

CERATOSAURUS
(seh-rat-oh-SORE-us)

CETIOSAURUS
(see-tee-oh-SORE-us)

CHASMOSAURUS
(kaz-moh-SORE-us)

COELOPHYSIS
(SEEL-oh-FIE-sis)

COMPSOGNATHUS
(komp-soh-NAY-thus)

CORYTHOSAURUS
(koh-rith-oh-SORE-us)

CRIORHYNCHUS
(cry-oh-RINK-us)

CRYPTOCLIDUS
(cript-oh-CLIE-dus)

DASPLETOSAURUS
(das-PLEE-toh-SORE-us)

DEINOCHEIRUS
(DINE-oh-KEE-rus)

DEINONYCHUS
(die-NON-i-kus)

DIMORPHODON
(die-MORF-oh-don)

DIPLODOCUS
(di-PLOH-de-kus)

DROMAEOSAURUS
(DROH-may-oh-SORE-us)

DROMICEIOMIMUS
(droh-MEE-see-oh-
MEEM-us)

EDMONTONIA
(ed-mon-TONE-ee-ah)

EDMONTOSAURUS
(ed-MON-toh-SORE-us)

EORAPTOR
(EE-oh-RAP-tor)

EUOPLOCEPHALUS
(you-op-loh-SEF-ah-lus)

EUSTREPTOSPONDYLUS
(yoo-STREP-toh-SPON-
die-lus)

GALLIMIMUS
(gal-lee-MEEM-us)

GRYPOSAURUS
(GRIPE-oh-SORE-us)

HADROSAURUS
(HAD-roh-SORE-us)

HERRERASAURUS
(eh-ray-rah-SORE-us)

HETERODONTOSAURUS
(HET-er-oh-DONT-oh-
SORE-us)

HYPACROSAURUS
(high-PAK-roh-SORE-us)

HYPSILOPHODON
(hip-sih-LOH-foh-don)

ICTHYOSAURUS
(IKH-thee-oh-SORE-us)

IGUANODON
(ig-WHA-noh-don)

INGENIA
(in-GAY-nee-a)

KENTROSAURUS
(KEN-troh-SORE-us)

LAMBEOSAURUS
(LAMB-ee-oh-SORE-us)

MAIASAURA
(MY-ah-SORE-ah)

MAMENCHISAURUS
(mah-MEN-chee-SORE-us)

MASOSAURUS
(MAZ-oh-SORE-us)

MASSOSPONDYLUS
(MAS-oh-SPON-die-lus)

MEGALOSAURUS
(MEG-ah-loh-SORE-us)

MELANOROSAURUS
(MEL-an-or-oh-SORE-us)

MURAENOSAURUS
(mure-rain-oh-SORE-us)

MUSSAURUS
(mus-OR-us)

MUTTABURRASAURUS
(MUT-a-BUR-a-SORE-us)

ORNITHOLESTES
(OR-nith-OH-LES-teez)

ORNITHOMIMUS
(OR-ni-thoh-MEE-mus)

OURANOSAURUS
(OO-ran-oh-SORE-us)

OVIRAPTOR
(OHV-ih-RAP-tor)

PACYCEPHALOSAURUS
(PAK-ee-SEF-a-loh-
SORE-US)

PARASAUROLOPHUS
(par-a-SORE-oh-LOAF-us)

PELONEUSTES
(pel-oh-nee-OOST-ees)

PINACOSAURUS
(pin-AK-oh-SORE-us)

PLATEOSAURUS
(PLAT-ee-oh-SORE-us)

PLIOSAURUS
(plie-oh-SORE-us)

POLACANTHUS
(pol-a-KAN-thus)

PRENOCEPHALE
(pren-oh-SEF-a-lee)

PSITTACOSAURUS
(Si-tak-oh-SORE-us)

PTERANODON
(teh-RANN-oh-don)

PTERODACTYLUS
(teh-roh-DACT-illus)

QUETZALCOATLUS
(kwet-zal-COAT-lus)

RHAMPHORHYNCHUS
(RAM-foh-RING-khus)

RIOJASAURUS
(ree-O-ha-SORE-us)

SALTASAURUS
(sal-te-SORE-us)

SAUROPELTA
(SORE-oh-PEL-ta)

SEISMOSAURUS
(SIZE-moh-SORE-us)

SHONISAURUS
(shon-ee-SORE-us)

SORDES
(SOHR-deez)

STEGOCERAS
(ste-GOS-er-as)

STEGOSAURUS
(STEG-oh-SORE-us)

STENOPTERYGIUS
(sten-OP-teh-RIDGE-ee-us)

STRUTHIOMIMUS
(STRUTH-ee-oh-
MEEM-us)

STYGIMOLOCH
(STIJ-i-MOH-lok)

STYRACOSAURUS
(sty-RAK-oh-SORE-us)

SUPERSAURUS
(SUE-per-SORE-us)

TOROSAURUS
(tor-oh-SORE-us)

TRICERATOPS
(try-SERRA-tops)

TROODON
(TROH-oh-don)

TUOJIANGOSAURUS
(toh-HWANG-oh-
SORE-us)

TYRANNOSAURUS
(tie-RAN-oh-SORE-us)

ULTRASAURUS
(ul-tra-SORE-us)

VELOCIRAPTOR
(vel-O-si-RAP-tor)

Glossary

AMPHIBIANS
A group of animals that are able to live both on land and in water.

ANKYLOSAURS
Quadrupedal, armoured ornithischians.

ARMOURED DINOSAURS
Dinosaurs whose bodies were protected by bony plates or spikes. These included ankylosaurs and some sauropods.

ARCHOSAUROMORPHS
A major group of reptiles which includes dinosaurs, thecodonts, pterosaurs, crocodiles, and birds.

BIPEDAL
Walking on the two hind legs only.

CARNIVORE
A meat-eating animal.

CARNOSAURS
A group of large theropods.

CERATOPSIANS
Quadrupedal ornithischians. Most ceratopsians had horns and frills on their heads.

CLASSIFICATION
The process of arranging animals into groups, related by common physical features.

COLD-BLOODED
Dependant on conditions outside the body for temperature regulation, such as the Sun's heat, to give warmth to the body.

CONIFERS
Trees which bear cones, such as pines and firs.

CONTINENTAL DRIFT
The constant movement of the plates which make up the Earth's crust.

CRETACEOUS PERIOD
The third period of the Mezozoic era – 65-145 million years ago.

DIAPSID
A reptile group which includes the archosauromorphs, the lepidosauromorphs, and the euryapsids.

DINOSAURS
An extinct group of archosauromorphs with an erect stance. They included the ancestors of modern birds.

DUCKBILLED DINOSAURS
Another name for the hadrosaurs.

EURYAPSID
A reptile group which includes the two groups of sea reptiles: plesiosaurs and ichthyosaurs.

EXTINCTION
The process by which living things die out of existence.

FOLIAGE
Leaves, twigs, and branches.

FOSSIL
The preserved remains of something that once lived.

GASTROLITHS
Stones that are swallowed to help grind up food in the stomach.

HADROSAURS
Large ornithopods with duck-like bills, of which there are two groups: lambeosaurines and hadrosaurines.

HERBIVORE
An animal which feeds on plants.

INVERTEBRATES
Animals without a backbone.

ISCHIUM
One of the two lower hipbones of dinosaurs (the other was the pubis). The ischium anchored muscles that worked the hind legs.

JURASSIC PERIOD
The second period of the Mesozoic era – 145-208 million years ago.

MESOZOIC ERA
The period of time between 65-245 million years ago. The Mesozoic era incorporated the Triassic, Jurassic, and Cretaceous periods.

ORNITHISCHIANS
The "bird-hipped" dinosaurs. One of the two major groups of dinosaurs.

ORNITHOPODS
Small to very large plant-eating ornithischians that were mostly bipedal.

PACHYCEPHALOSAURS
Bipedal ornithopods. Also known as bone-headed dinosaurs, because the roof of their skull was very thick.

PALAEONTOLOGIST
A person who studies fossils.

PROSAUROPODS
Small to large early sauropodomorphs.

PTEROSAURS
The flying reptiles of the Mesozoic era. Distant cousins of the dinosaurs.

PUBIS
One of the two lower hipbones of dinosaurs (the other was the ischium). In some dinosaurs, the pubis anchored the muscle that pulled the hind legs forwards.

QUADRUPEDAL
Walking on all four legs.

REPTILES
A group of "cold-blooded" vertebrates with scaly skin.

SAURISCHIANS
The "lizard-hipped" dinosaurs. One of the two major groups of dinosaurs.

SAUROPODOMORPHS
A group of quadrupedal herbivorous dinosaurs with long tails and necks. This group included the largest land animals that ever lived.

SAUROPODS
Large to immense sauropodomorphs.

STEGOSAURS
Quadrupedal ornithischians with two rows of plates and/or spines running along the neck, back, and tail.

SYNAPSID
A reptile group which includes mammal-like reptiles (reptiles which are distantly related to mammals).

THECODONTS
A group of archosauromorphs which are the ancestors of the dinosaurs.

THEROPODS
Bipedal, carnivorous saurischian dinosaurs.

TRIASSIC PERIOD
The first period of the Mesozoic era – 208-245 million years ago.

VERTEBRAE
Bones of the spinal column.

VERTEBRATES
Animals with backbones.

WARM-BLOODED
Maintaining body warmth by turning the energy gained by food into heat.

Index

Acknowledgements

Dorling Kindersley would like to thank:

Hilary Bird for the index. Esther Labi and Robert Graham for editorial assistance. Carnegie Museum of Natural History for use of *Apatosaurus* skeleton on pages 90/91.

Photographs by:

Paul Bricknell, Andy Crawford, John Douns, Lynton Gardiner, Steve Gorton, Colin Keates, Gary Kevin, Dave King, William Lindsay, Ray Moller, Miguel Periera, Tim Ridley, Dave Rudlan, Bruce Selyen, Paul Sereno, Harry Taylor, Jerry Young

Illustrations by:

Roby Braun, Lynn Chadwick, Simone End, Eugene Fleury, Giuliano Fornari, Steve Kirk, Janos Marffy, Ikkyu Murakawa, Andrew Robinson, Graham Rosewarne, John Sibbick, John Temperton, John Woodcock.

Picture credits: t = top b = bottom c = centre l= left r = right
American Natural History Museum 140tl; 141 cl, Roby Braun 66tr.
Fortean 126tl.
Frank Lane Picture Library/Eric and David Hosking 55tr.

Hulton Picture Library 18tl; 138tl.
Image Bank/Robert Hardrie 135tl.
Kobal 23tl. Ikkyu Murakawa 114cl; 114cr.
Museum of the Rockies/Bruce Selyem 57tr; 76 77c; 150tl; 150bl; 150r; 151l; 151tr; 151br.
Natural History Museum, London 23br; 102cr; 105tl; 136.
Science Photo Library/Julian Baum 134 bl. John Sereno 58tr. John Sibbick 55br; 106bl.

Every effort has been made to trace the copyright holders and we apologise in advance for any unintentional omissions. We would be pleased to insert the appropriate acknowledgement in any subsequent edition of this publication.